# A LETTER TO MY
# FORMER SELF

### THE LOVE SHE MOST DESIRED AND THE RESPECT HE DESPERATELY NEEDED

## MIGUEL & BLANCA QUINONES

Copyright © 2017 by Miguel & Blanca Quinones

All rights reserved. No part of this publication may be reproduced, distributed, or transmitted in any form or by any means, including photocopying, recording, or other electronic or mechanical methods, without the prior written permission of the publisher, except in the case of brief quotations embodied in critical reviews and certain other noncommercial uses permitted by copyright law.

ISBN 13: 978-1-63616-256-0

eBook ISBN: 978-1-63616-257-7

Published by Opportune Independent Publishing Company

Edited by Katherine Adams

Printed in the United States of America

For permission requests, write to the publisher, addressed "Attention: Permissions Coordinator" to the address below.

info@opportunepublishing.com

www. opportunepublishing.com

# TABLE OF CONTENTS

What do you think you know about abusive relationships?

CHAPTER ONE: Blanca: My Beginning    1

    My Role in the Family
    My First Attack
    Daniel
    Hiding My Pregnancy
    You're Nobody
    Keeping My Head Down
    The Baby's Birth
    Daniel Returns
    Standing Alone
    Oscar
    Meeting Miguel
    The Real Miguel
    Drugs and Depression
    My Rock Bottom

CHAPTER TWO: Miguel's Beginning    21

    From Golden Boy to Tough Guy
    Building a Reputation
    Getting in Trouble
    Sex and Drugs
    Childhood Role Models
    Meeting Blanca
    The Proposal
    Drug Overdose
    My Rock Bottom
    Divine Intervention
    Relapse and Change

CHAPTER THREE: Blanca: Starting Over Alone    37

    Miguel's Illness
    The First Sign of Change
    Persistent Doubts

    Holding My Breath
    More Signs of Change
    The Next Step
    Establishing Trust
    Good Influences

CHAPTER FOUR: Miguel: Beginning My Recovery     49

    Becoming a Real Man
    Changing My Perspective
    Introspection and More Change
    The New Miguel
    Financial Responsibility
    Changes in the Marriage
    Getting on Track and Staying on Track

CHAPTER FIVE: Blanca: Carrying the Family Again     63

    Dealing with Setbacks…and Anger
    Suck it Up Again
    Finding My Way
    A New Profession and a New Outlook
    There's So Much More Out There

CHAPTER SIX: Miguel: Getting Off My Back and On My Feet     71

    New Job, Old Messages in My Head
    Positive Words
    Inspiration from the Bible
    Living My Accomplishments
    Teaching Others What I Learned
    Helping Others Find their Way
    All This Will Be Added Unto You
    Action and Example

CHAPTER SEVEN: Miguel Today: Attitude     83

    The Future
    Raising a Son
    Blanca Today: A Drastic Change in My Head
    Finding Women to Speak Life into your Life

CHAPTER EIGHT: Raising My Daughter     89

# *WHAT DO YOU THINK YOU KNOW ABOUT ABUSIVE RELATIONSHIPS?*

Only a fragile, powerless woman would stay in an abusive relationship. A woman who stays with her abuser lacks intelligence. She is weak, and that's why she allows herself to be abused. She puts up with it partly because she feels she has no choice, and partly because she is too ashamed to admit that it's happening to her. It doesn't matter if a woman seems to be strong and in control of her life. If she stays with her abuser, it's her own choice. She should just leave. If it's so bad, why doesn't she just leave? Right? Wrong.

An abusive man must have had an abusive father. Only men who see their fathers strike their mothers grow up to do that. A man like that can't control his rage. He's charming one minute and a monster the next. Right? Not always.

How do intelligent, competent people end up in violent, abusive relationships? We learned, after we'd come through our violent courtship and marriage, that the foundation was set early for both of us. Both of us, in our own particular dysfunctional way, found the partner who mirrored the way we felt about ourselves at the time.

This is the story of two people who lost their way…and found it again. This is a road map for those who are struggling in an abusive relationship, with the assurance that if both sides are willing to work, there is a way out. This is not a story about waiting and hoping for the abusive person to change. We learned that in order for our lives to be different, we both had to make different choices or nothing would ever get better.

We went through this nightmare, and now we are speaking to you from the other side.

# CHAPTER ONE

## *BLANCA: MY BEGINNING*

I did not witness violence of any kind in my home during my childhood. I was born the ninth of eleven children in Mexico, but since the age of seven, I was raised in Oklahoma, and later moved to Kansas. My mother passed away of cancer at that time, and our dad raised us on his own. He never left us. I have a great dad. But even though I knew my dad loved me and I was well provided for, I can look back and see clearly how I was set on a path that led me toward a rape, a pregnancy by one violent criminal, followed by another pregnancy and marriage to a man that had all the classic earmarks of an abuser: a terrible temper, a serious drinking problem, and frequent jealousy-fueled rages that usually ended with a fight, an arrest, and a trip to jail.

I think often about the fact that I didn't have a mother growing up. I always felt it was so unfair. The other kids I knew all had mothers, but I didn't. I had five sisters and five brothers. I knew my place in the family. My sisters and I were there to serve our father and our brothers. My job was to cook, clean, and even prepare my dad's bath and lay out his clothes when he got home. I cleaned my brothers' rooms and did their laundry. It was the girls' responsibility to do these things, not theirs.

### *MY ROLE IN THE FAMILY*

I accepted my role without question—the men were dominant, and I was there to serve. If it needed to be done, I just did it. And as life went on, and as each of my older sisters left the house and got married, it was the next sister's responsibility to take up her work. It was my job to just adapt—a skill that regrettably, I mastered very well.

None of my decisions were my own. My father or brothers told me what to do, and my older sisters even decided what I should wear. I had no opinions, and as I look back on myself, I'm sad to say I didn't know I could have a dream for myself. I went to school, played sports, and was a cheerleader. I did my schoolwork and I had my friends, but I always fulfilled my responsibilities at home.

Perhaps if I'd had a mother, I might have had some guidance and learned the things that I now know that mothers teach their daughters, but I was raised in survival mode. I knew nothing of the conversations my friends were surely having with their mothers about everything from the simple to the complicated. The natural changes in my body during puberty came as a complete shock to me—not even my sisters enlightened me. No one told me I had value beyond my housekeeping duties, and no one displayed any interest in my opinion or my feelings.

I never talked about not having a mom, but I always felt I was somehow less valuable because I didn't have one. There's something about not having a mother that makes a young girl feel uncomfortable down to her core. To this day, I feel there is a void in my life because I do not have a mother.

## *MY FIRST ATTACK*

Now I can see that I was searching for someone to love me, affirm my value, and accept me. As a teenage girl growing up in a very small, rural town in Kansas, I was close to the kids in my high school class—all eight of them. We were all good friends, or so I believed. When I was 16, I went to a house party where alcohol was served. I knew I wasn't supposed to drink, but I did and I got a little tipsy. A boy from my school took me down to a tornado cellar, and I went willingly with him.

Before I knew it, he was raping me. My protests and cries of "No!" were ignored, and when he was done, I was so weak; I couldn't have pushed him off me if I'd tried. Finally, I crawled up the steps of the storm cellar, crying, and even scraped my knees. I went home and told no one for three days.

When I finally told my brother what happened, he looked for the boy, took him out into a field and beat him up. Nothing else happened. I went back to school and saw him and it was as if nothing happened. I felt the episode was my fault. I shouldn't have been drinking. I shouldn't have gone into the cellar with him. I blamed myself for being in that situation and carried the shame of that incident locked away deep inside myself.

## *DANIEL*

Three years later, I moved to Rosenberg, Texas with my sister and enrolled in school. It was a huge change for me. In Kansas, the majority of the school was white, with maybe four Hispanic students. When I walked in the school in Rosenberg, I was overwhelmed. There were hundreds of students and I thought, I can't do this!

I met a man named Daniel who seemed nice, but I didn't know much about him. I had a brief relationship with him but ended it once I found out he was heavily involved with drug dealing. I didn't want anything to do with that kind of lifestyle. To get away from him, I moved to Houston.

Four months after my brief relationship with Daniel, I began to feel strange. I was so naïve and no one had taught me any lessons about relationships between men and women, so it never dawned on me that I could be pregnant. I'd learned nothing about valuing my body from any of my sisters or even from my father. I had not been taught about respect, or love, or to how to be a good example from home.

No one ever said, "Wait till you find a guy with a good job who went to college and will treat you with respect." So now, I was in complete disbelief. I was pregnant by a drug addict who remains to this day in prison for drug-related offenses and assault to a police officer.

## *HIDING MY PREGNANCY*

When I came to the shocking realization that I was pregnant, I hid it for a while, but ultimately confided my secret to the sister with whom I was living in Houston. I was very frightened about her response, so I decided to tell her as I was stepping out of the car when she drove me to work. That way she couldn't yell at me or throw me out of the car.

But she did yell at me. She told me I was an embarrassment to the family and kept asking me how I could have done such a thing. She told me I'd have to do what frightened me the most—tell my father. Soon, I retreated into a bedroom at my sister's house and stayed there for an entire week, emerging only to eat when she left the house. I was so embarrassed and ashamed. My sister called my father and told him to come to her house.

When my father arrived, I had no choice but to tell him I was pregnant. His response was that I should get married. I told him I didn't love the baby's father, nor did I want to marry him, and he said if that was the case, I shouldn't have done this. He wept, asking me repeatedly how I could have shamed our family this way. I felt a sense of complete failure.

I had no place to go. At this point, I was about six months' pregnant. Daniel eventually found me and started to call, but for a long time, I never answered him. I finally decided to answer Daniel's phone call one day and told him that I was pregnant. Right away he asked me to move in with him. At first, I said no.

But then, when I realized I didn't have any alternatives, I thought it might be my only hope. I shared with one of my brothers that Daniel wanted me to live with him. Daniel said he was coming to get me. I packed all my things and waited on the curb for Daniel to pick me up. He never showed up. The embarrassment and the rejection of this came over me. He didn't show up! Even though I didn't want to go with him, he had been my only hope. I just kept thinking, how am I going to take care of this baby?

My brother came out and asked me if I wanted him to help me to bring my things back into my sister's house. I just cried and cried. I couldn't look at my brother in the face.

### *YOU'RE NOBODY*

I thought things were going to get better for me when my other brother came a few days later with his wife and kids and asked me to stay with him. I got so excited, and I was glad I had a place to go. I went and stayed with him. His wife knew how my family felt about my pregnancy. She was really ugly to me. I thought she was jealous because my brother was giving me a lot of attention. He was very sweet to me, and she hated that.

They got into a lot of arguments about me, and one night, they had a really bad argument and she went and slept on my bed where I was sleeping just so I wouldn't have a bed to sleep in. So, I sat outside all night till about 4 a.m. and I don't know why, but my brother came out. He asked, "why are you out here?" I said, "I have no place to sleep. She is sleeping on my bed." So, he said, "come and sleep with me on my bed." We slept on the bed together, and the next morning he told me to not come out of the room till he came home from work. As soon as he left, his wife came in and told me that I had to leave right away. She grabbed me by the arms and pinned me against the wall.

She was yelling at me, literally in my face. She told me that no one loved me and she called me a slut. She said that not even my family wanted me, and she called me a nobody. She was so ugly to me. I couldn't move, so I bit her hand so hard, my teeth marks are probably still there! She finally let go, but we pushed each other on the bed, and her sister walked in and she made her let me go. So she walked out still yelling at me. That's when I locked the door.

They had a phone in their bedroom and it rang. I was hoping it was someone from my family. It was my sister that lived out of state. She asked me how I was doing. And I said I was fine. I didn't tell her what just happened to me. But my voice cracked and again she asked, "what's wrong?" I began to cry and told her what happened.

She told me that she would get someone to come for me. Soon after, another sister showed up to get me. At the time, my dad and younger sister Dora were staying with the sister that came to get me. It was so hard because they wouldn't let Dora talk to me because they thought I was a bad influence, but Dora wrote letters to me and said that she loved me and that she would help me. Dora was very supportive.

### *KEEPING MY HEAD DOWN*

When my sister picked me up and took me away from there, I had no maternity clothes so I had to cut my jeans just so they would fit. My sister took me to the mall, and the entire time there I walked with my head down. I was so ashamed about the way I looked. My dad was still not talking to me. I cried every night. One day my dad came in and told me to stop crying. He said, "what's done is done." My dad ended up buying a home and I went to live with him, my sister Dora and my brother Jesus.

If this was not enough shame and embarrassment throughout this time, Daniel somehow got my telephone number and began to call again. But it was short lived, so I thought, because he ended up in prison yet again for another offense. But he still managed to call from prison. Then when he was released he went looking for me and my daughter, it was very scary. Then a few years later, he went back to prison and has not been out since then.

### *THE BABY'S BIRTH*

The day my daughter was born, I had no idea what was going to happen. The doctor advised me to be induced because the baby was about a week late. I didn't even know what "induce" meant. One of my brothers was very supportive, and he dropped me off at the hospital at 6 in the morning. I had nothing but a little Walmart bag with some things in it. He went to work and I walked in by myself. A nurse came up to me and said, "you're having a baby!" She walked me to where I needed to go. They put me in a room and prepared me for birth. I was all alone but I was not emotional or crying. I was just trying to be strong. I kept saying to myself, "I did this to myself. It's my fault that I am here and this is happening to me. Suck it up."

I was terribly hungry. My sister Dora came after school with my brother, and asked if I was OK. I wasn't going to say I was in pain or hungry. I was just trying not to be a bother to anyone so they left. The pains came harder and harder. I didn't understand about an epidural. I didn't know anything about childbirth. I didn't sign anything about pain medication because I didn't understand it, and the pain was so bad. I just wanted to run. The pain was much worse than anything I ever imagined.

About 2 in the morning, the nurse told me that the doctor was on his way and she instructed me not to push. I thought I was going to die. They took me into the delivery room. I was so scared but the nurse there was being so helpful. She would rub my back and encourage me to keep me going. I started pushing and suddenly my little sister Dora walked in. She said she couldn't sleep and she felt like she had to come. So, she helped me through the delivery. I remember leaving bruises on her arms. It was so painful. I tore and they had to cut me. I had so many stitches. And that was that. That is how my baby Briana was born.

I ended up coming home and I remember thinking that I didn't want the baby to cry because I didn't want to be a bother. I didn't want my dad to hear the baby cry. I tried to breastfeed but it hurt too much. So, my brother went out of his way to buy my baby formula. The very next morning, everyone had already left for work and school, I was all alone and couldn't even walk because of my stitches due to the tearing when delivering my baby. I was bleeding so badly. I tried to keep myself clean, but it was so hard and I was in so much pain.

One day, very soon after the baby was born, there was a knock at the door, and it was an older lady doing door to door evangelism. I actually invited her in. It was so great for me at that moment, having her there. She listened to me and talked to me. Before, we never answered the door to any religious groups, but at that moment, they seemed like the only ones who cared. They came in, they wanted to see the baby. For a while they kept coming and I always looked forward to it.

## *DANIEL RETURNS*

It took me a long time to recover. About a month later, a friend invited me to the park. She wanted me to get out of the house. I remember driving towards the park and all of a sudden, there was a car coming at us and then blocked us. My friend said, don't look! But of course, I looked, and it was Daniel, Briana's biological father. He got out of the car and came right to Briana's side of the car. I jumped out of the car. I didn't know what he was going to do.

Daniel picked up his shirt and he showed me he had a gun in his waistband. I got so scared and got back in the car. I tried to close the door but he stuck his hand in there and I said MOVE! I slammed the door on his hand. Finally, he took his hand out and he left. We went home, but he would still drive around the house and call. I never answered. I never wanted anything more to do with him.

## *STANDING ALONE*

My brother Jesus helped me financially with Briana a lot. He bought diapers and baby necessities. He even paid for childcare costs for her so I could go to school and work for a certificate in secretarial and office administration. I had a friend who took me to school every day. It was good to have her. She encouraged me to continue, and I did.

When I finished my school, I got a job. Then I started being able to do it on my own. By the time I knew it, I had been doing it alone for three years. I worked very hard, and I was able to get good jobs. It was so hard but I would continue to take new challenges. I worked for an attorney, an oil and gas company, and Electric Company. I kept doing better and better. But I can honestly say that for those three years it was very hard.

With no emotional or financial support from Daniel, we had a very long way to go from the time of Briana's birth, but we are much better off without him. She still occasionally hears from him from prison.

## *OSCAR*

By the time I was 20, I was living with my daughter in Rosenberg in my father's house. I was dating a very nice young man named Oscar, who truly cared about my daughter and me. Still, I didn't bring him around much. I didn't want to let him come too close. He was my boyfriend, but I felt more that he was a good friend—very supportive, stable, and responsible.

Oscar had gone to school and had a good job. He was a good, dependable man. We dated for about two years and I finally got engaged to him, although I didn't really tell anyone about that. I ended up picking fights with him for no reason and one day, I threw my ring at him. I'm not sure why I didn't want to marry him, but I didn't. I always said that whoever married him would be very happy, but it was not going to be me.

## *MEETING MIGUEL*

I was still engaged to Oscar when I met Miguel. I was working as a secretary and I had a new car and I was out showing it off to my friends. As we drove, some of the girls pointed out a huge, ugly van driving beside me, but the driver was good looking! We began laughing. They said, look, he's turning! You should turn. So, I turned and he got out of the van where he lived, and he waved at us. My girlfriends were screaming, look, he waved! Just go around the block and go by his house again!

So, I did. I stopped in the middle of the road and went into his driveway. I didn't want to speak to him, but he came around to my side of the car and began asking questions. I didn't tell him I was engaged or that I had a child. He seemed like a bad boy, but strong—like he could protect me. He had a handsome, rough look and I guess I was attracted to that. He asked for my number, and I gave it to him but he never called.

At this time, in 1998, we still had phone books. I tracked down his number and called him so I could come clean about having a boyfriend and a child. Miguel was cocky. His reply was, "why are you talking to me if you have a boyfriend?" I told him I just wanted to come clean about it. I had a bad taste in my mouth about his attitude. But then, even after I told him I had a boyfriend and a baby, he asked me out on a date - I accepted his invitation.

Miguel took me to a steakhouse, and my daughter started coughing because she had not been feeling well. I told him I didn't feel comfortable and perhaps we needed to leave to get her some cough medicine. We took our food to go and stopped at a Walgreen's for cough medicine, which he paid for. I noticed he bought himself an apple juice to drink. I thought, he's so nice, and he's not a drinker! He seemed very nice to me.

I began wrestling with the problem of what to do about Oscar. We were still engaged, but I was attracted to Miguel. I started to be purposely mean and ugly to Oscar in the hopes that he would break up with me, but he would just cry and would ask me why I was hurting him. He would get so hurt when I tried to break up with him. At the same time, I noticed that Miguel was rude, jealous, overprotective, and he frightened me. Then he would be loving and caring and sweet. I didn't understand how he could be so good, yet so mean.

Finally, Oscar found out I was dating Miguel and that's when I took off my ring and threw it at him, trying to make him break up with me so I wouldn't have to break up with him. Oscar and I never officially broke up, but I began seeing Miguel exclusively.

## *THE REAL MIGUEL*

For a year, we dated off and on. His moods were either very hot or very cold. He was very jealous—always fighting with someone because he thought they might be staring at me. He was a very heavy drinker. He pushed and shoved me frequently while we were dating, and he had the foulest mouth I'd ever heard. All those things should have been a red flag. I never saw pushing or shoving in my home, and no one ever cursed in my family so this was all new to me. Despite all the pushing and shoving, he never actually hit or slapped me, and he was very sweet to my daughter.

I knew this wasn't right. I knew he shouldn't talk this way and I knew he shouldn't push me. I'd seen a neighbor of ours being abused by her husband when I was a child. I never understood how someone could put up with that. I believed I would never put up with that. But eventually, I was also putting up with it and I hid it very well. I never told anyone in my family that I was being treated this way.

We were both 23 when we got married and I had strong hesitations beforehand. Three days prior to the date, I tore up the marriage license and told him I didn't want to marry him. He let me know I would marry him, whether I liked it or not.

He was right. I'd just found out I was pregnant again. If I didn't marry him, I would disappoint and embarrass my father for a second time. They would tell me again I'd chosen this. In my mind, I was still the naïve girl who'd gotten herself pregnant by a drug dealer she barely knew. I still sometimes feel like that today. I was pregnant, so I had to get married. But on my wedding day, even though I was a not-very-happy pregnant bride, I believed that the baby and I would make him change. There was no way he'd abuse me while I was pregnant.

Of course, I was wrong. The abuse continued and even escalated when I was pregnant with my son Isaiha. Miguel's rages were set off by everything and anything. If I asked him where he'd been when he came home, or if he didn't like his home cooked meal, he'd fly into a rage. If he didn't like what I'd cooked, he would throw the plates or hit me with a pan. He hit me where you couldn't see the bruises—in my hair or on my back. If I questioned him about anything, he would slap me. He would pin me to the bed and hit me while I was pregnant. Once, he threw me and I landed on my back on a bed rail. I couldn't scream because it knocked the air out of me. It frightened him so much that he held me and said he was sorry.

And all that time, I never defended myself. I never cried for help, and I never let anyone know. I was the smallest person in the world. I went to the grocery store and looked at the other women and wondered if they could see what I was living. Miguel's family knew he had a history of violence and I assumed they knew what was going on, but they never asked. I wasn't about to tell anyone.

I would even try to leave. I would tell him, "I am leaving." His response was, "there's the door!" But then, as I went to open the door, he would get in front of me, close it, and laugh cruelly in my face. He said I wasn't going anywhere. I did call my sister-in law once, fearing for my life. She came and I ran to the neighbor's apartment with both of my kids. I stayed there, but only for a day. I went back because he promised he would not hit me anymore. Immediately, everything started back up again. This was my life for two years.

Miguel could not keep a job, I was the only one working. He was constantly drinking, hanging out with his buddies and not going to work. I took on the responsibility of paying bills and buying food. He would say he wanted to change. He thought, as soon as he can make $500 a week, we would be fine.

### *DRUGS AND DEPRESSION*

I remember that not long after our marriage, Miguel went to the emergency room for a drug overdose. I had no idea he was abusing cocaine. I filled out the forms in the hospital. They asked if he drank or smoked cigarettes. I said, yes. The questionnaire asked if he did drugs. Very confidently, I checked the NO box. I didn't believe he was on drugs.

That's when I learned the truth about his drug use. I was heavily pregnant. I was so embarrassed and deeply ashamed. How could I allow myself to get this low and allow something like this in my life? Everything just kept getting worse. I felt like I just had to take it and hope he stops. He told me that it was his first time he using cocaine and I believed him. He said he just didn't know what it would do to him. He appeared to be afraid knowing he could have died and I really thought he wouldn't use cocaine again. He came home and everything continued.

I was really spiraling downward. I felt like I was just getting smaller and smaller, down to nothing. I began to cut my hair with a knife. I don't know why, but I cut it over the sink in the kitchen. I don't even remember having any emotion while I was doing it. I just wanted to feel something, but I didn't.

All I can remember is feeling so much shame. I hated myself. I would hit my head on the wall and the floor. I was abusing myself. I never thought about suicide, but I remember thinking, what if I fall down the stairs? I just wanted to hurt myself because I was so angry at how I could allow myself to live this way. I began to hit back because I wanted to hurt us both. I thought, this is all my fault. I believed the problems were because of me. Mentally, I was not there. I was experiencing a horrible sense of depression and shame and I didn't know how to make anything better.

Because of Miguel's addiction, we were without lights and without food sometimes. I went to apply for government assistance. I had never been through this before. My family had never used government assistance. I asked myself, "how low have I become?" We were eating crackers and cheese. The new car I had been driving was repossessed. Miguel always had warrants for his arrest for failure to appear in court, unpaid tickets, fighting. He was always in and out of jail. I often used our rent money to bail him out. Everything was going downhill and I was miserable and couldn't live this way anymore.

That's when I decided that it was time for me to start fighting back. I got to the point where I wanted him to hit me so I could hit him back. I began provoking him. I remember driving on the freeway and he was drinking beer. I thought, this is my chance to hit him because he can't go anywhere. I took a beer bottle and hit him with it while he was driving and punched him. I thought, I am really going to get it when we get home. But when we got there, he didn't do anything. And so, I thought it was right to hit him and I shouldn't be afraid.

## *MY ROCK BOTTOM*

One of the worst moments was when we were both driving in our separate cars, with the kids in the back seat of the car I was driving. He was screaming and laughing at me, and I was so angry, I hit him head on with my car. I didn't fear him anymore, and I had lost all respect. He threatened to call the police and I said, "What are you going to tell them, that I hit my own car?" Both cars were under my name. I left the house for the day so things would calm down.

Not long after that, we got into another huge fight. I said to myself, that's it! Miguel was laughing at me in such a mocking and ugly way. I picked up his steel-toed construction boot and threw it at him, as hard as I could. At that moment, my four-year-old daughter walked in front of me and I hit her with it instead.

That was the end. I had reached my rock bottom. I told Miguel he had to leave.

# CHAPTER TWO

## *MIGUEL'S BEGINNING*

As I look back at my life, I can see exactly where things started to go wrong for me. I was born and raised in Rosenberg, Texas, in a two-parent home, the middle child of five siblings. I was the first son, which as it turns out, didn't necessarily work in my favor.

The way I was brought up, the male was the dominant figure of the house. There was no questioning that. The women did all the "woman" things like cooking and cleaning and raising the kids. My father was the head of the house hold and my mother accepted that. As I can recall, there wasn't much conflict in the house because everyone accepted the way things were. There was no violence between my parents.

I had two older sisters, so when I was born a boy, (the long-awaited boy for my father), I was very spoiled. Maybe more than spoiled. I would say I was overly babied and indulged—to the extreme. I didn't start walking till I was almost two years old because my mother always held me. She didn't want me to fall down and hurt myself like scraping my knees.

My father was the same way with me but in a different kind of way. He always made sure that I had the best clothes and even jewelry! I have seen baby pictures of myself wearing rings, necklaces, and bracelets. It was a lot! When I had my first birthday party, my parents invited so many people and had a huge Mexican fiesta, complete with a butchered cow. Throughout the years, I have heard many stories from my family about how spoiled I was. Some would even say that it was really too much. I can't really say that my mother didn't spoil my siblings but one thing is for sure, I was spoiled much more than they were. I remember not being disciplined in any way. I was the golden child—the firstborn son.

As I got a little older, I began to develop a very bad attitude and temper. I was four years old when my next younger brother was born, but I made sure I stayed the golden boy. On his first birthday party, I totally ruined it for him. I threw temper tantrums and made everyone sing happy birthday to me instead of for him. For the first time in my life, it wasn't all about me, and I was very angry about it. Everyone sang to me and thought my behavior was funny and cute.

I always threw major temper tantrums if I didn't get my way. I wanted my way and I didn't stop until I got it. I remember when I was five or six, there was an occasion that might have planted a very bad idea in my head. I remember that I was angry and I wanted to punch my sister Claudia, but she was bigger and stronger. So, I quickly ran to my mom and she asked, "What's the matter?" I responded, "I want to punch my sister but she won't let me!" My mother said to Claudia, "Why don't you just let him punch you?" So, I then proceeded to punch her on her shoulder. I probably couldn't even reach that high. But after that I felt satisfied. I got it out of my system. I learned that punching was an acceptable way of getting what I wanted, and that's a "lesson" that did a lot of damage to my life as I grew older.

## *FROM GOLDEN BOY TO TOUGH GUY*

When my youngest brother Christian was born, I was ten years old. By this time, I was trying less to be the golden boy. Now I was trying to develop a "tough guy" persona. This is when I began to make friends with people I shouldn't have been with. I also hung around with a lot of my older cousins. At this age, I began smoking pot and drinking.

No one was supervising us and no one knew what we were doing. We were just a few boys having fun, so I thought. Going to the woods hunting rabbits, climbing trees and just hanging out with the boys. But in the middle of that we would spark up a joint or two and get high. I didn't do this because I felt neglected by my mother. She was very loving and caring to me. Although my temper was very bad, she could never imagine in a million years that I was doing drugs and drinking alcohol at such a young age. I guess knowing that my mother would never think this of me, I could hide it better. My mother would sometimes hear from others that I was smoking and drinking but she refused to admit to herself that I was doing these things. She would deny it. It set the foundation for a lot of problems that came later.

My father is a great man and he worked hard to support us. He always lectured me about my behavior. I remember him always telling me not to end up a drug addict. Both my parents loved me and wanted the best for me, but many years later, when I was rushed to the hospital for a cocaine overdose, my mother finally admitted that she knew those people were telling the truth. She accepted what she didn't want to believe, because she couldn't deny it any more. She could not believe that her baby boy was laying in a hospital bed because of a drug overdose.

I remember clearly the first time I got drunk. I was ten years old and I was walking home from a friend's house. They were feeding me jalapeños so I could sober up. They walked me home and helped sneak me in my house. Sneaking in and out of my bedroom window was a frequent thing. It was easy to hide what I was doing. My father was always working and my mother was busy raising my younger brothers.

At this point, my sisters were old enough to help my younger brothers in their pursuit of sports. Now I watched as my little brothers got to play. My sisters were too young to help me in this area when I was a kid. I would have loved to play sports too, but

I'm pretty sure my mother was worried that if I played, I might fall and hurt myself, so I never played.

I feel like I missed out on a lot because of that. But despite how my mother felt, I did play baseball one year when I was older, but I was terrible because I didn't have the earlier years of playing like the other kids did. They made fun of me a lot. I wasn't a very good player. I was afraid to get hit with the ball. I remember one time after a game, the kids were talking about me because I played poorly. I walked to get my free snow cone after the game and I went to a secluded area and I cried because I was so hurt. When I was done crying, I felt this anger come upon me. I wanted to hurt someone to get this anger out of me but I didn't. This was the only year I played and I didn't want to play anymore. I believe this incident planted a really bad thought in my head and it played a huge role as to why I was so mean to people from that point on.

## *BUILDING A REPUTATION*

During this time, I moved into what I thought was my role as "older brother." I felt I had to be very protective and very hard. I decided that I wanted people to fear me. My dad worked so much, and my brothers and I would be out playing and I wanted them to learn, but something would arise and I would feel like I had to jump in and protect them.

I felt that I had to keep up this reputation I had created for being very hard, and to build on it even more. I liked that people were afraid of me. By the time I was 14, I started picking fights. I just wanted to be the Big Bad Brother. I was getting very good at that role.

When I walked into a room, the atmosphere changed. I liked that my presence would make people nervous or afraid to speak for fear that I would think they were saying something about me. I became good at making something out of nothing. No one could look at me without risking a fight. I took everything as antagonism. I was becoming a real thug. Today, I look back on that time and I hate those memories.

Even though I was a thuggish boy, my grades were surprisingly good in school. I believe that my good academics fooled my parents a bit. I'm sure they thought, "well his grades look good so he must be doing good." But then my grades slowly declined, but it's because I was hanging around even worse kids than before. I was still drinking heavily and smoking pot all the time, and by my junior year in high school, I started doing cocaine. By this time, I think they knew at home what I was doing. I got home very late most of the time. They knew I was drinking, but they didn't know about the drugs—maybe they just didn't want to know or accept it. I came from a typical Mexican household. The males could do whatever they wanted.

### *GETTING IN TROUBLE*

My father would often tell me to be careful and to not get into "trouble." For him, the definition of "trouble" was going to jail. Despite the lecturing from my dad, I did go to jail on many occasions. The first time was for fighting. The fight occurred at a public event so I was charged for misconduct and resisting arrest. I was only in jail overnight because my mother ran to my aide and bailed me out. Being in jail really didn't have much of an effect on me.

The fact that jail didn't impact me was very negative for my overall attitude. It made me feel that I'd had a taste of jail and it made me even more of a tough guy. Obviously, that meant I was super tough. So what if I mess up again? I had seen jail and I was not scared of it. I thought I was really cool and bad, and I was proud of that.

I wanted to quit high school as a senior. I did not like being in classrooms. I felt like I just needed to be out having fun and being bad to help my reputation. I asked if there was a way to test out of school and to my surprise they were going to have a GED testing class the next day, so I took the test and got my GED. I thought, "So what? I got my diploma, what's the big deal?" It wasn't important to me. I look back and I can still see my mother's disappointment.

## *SEX AND DRUGS*

After quitting high school, my dad pushed me a lot. He said I had to go to work if I didn't want to go to school. He worked construction, so I went to work with him. I didn't like it at all. I was 17 and construction was hard. I thought, there must be something better than this. Even though my life choices were so bad, I still had a good head on my shoulders for school. I went to technical college and ended up with an associate's degree in electronics engineering.

The entire time I was in college, I was still drinking, smoking pot, and doing all sorts of drugs. I was sporadically employed because I couldn't hold a job. I was always under the influence. I missed a lot of Mondays and sometimes Tuesdays because of my partying.

I'd developed another reputation to uphold, besides my "tough guy" image. I was known to be a womanizer/player. I had been in and out of a lot of relationships. I didn't care much about any of the women; it was just about sex for me. I would always have one relationship that I considered my "main" girlfriend. But there were always other women. I was never faithful to any woman.

I had lots of women of different races. I loved women and I had to have sex! I would travel many miles to meet up with women. I had them all over Texas, from Houston, Dallas, Lubbock and San Antonio. There came a point where I didn't even have to work because the women I had would pay for all my necessities. They loved me and I felt really good about that.

But then I had a very close call! The Fort Bend Health Department came looking for me. When they found me, they apprehended me and told me it was urgent that I went with them to their clinic. A woman had given them my full name as one of the men she had sex with. I was never told what I was being tested for but I thank GOD every day that the tests came back negative. The fear was short lived. I started back up with the relationships I already had.

## CHILDHOOD ROLE MODELS

When I was a little boy, I saw that drinking and "machismo" were closely associated among the men in my family. We would have family and friends come over to our house just about every weekend. The men would be gathered together while the women would gather together at a distance or go inside. I remember those times as a little kid, walking behind them where they sat and they'd set their beers on the ground. I would go and take little drinks out of their beers. No one thought that was a problem. In fact, they thought it was funny. I listened to them talk. Who can outdo the others? Who can drink the most? Who had the most women?

I was brought up around this behavior for most of my life. Every man had his "reputation" to uphold. To them, watching me drink beer was making our name great. They said, "That's my boy!" I thought that by imitating their behavior, I was making them proud of me. So, by the time I met Blanca, my life was a total mess.

## MEETING BLANCA

Around the time when I met Blanca I was drinking heavily and doing all kinds of drugs. I will never forget the day I met her, I was just coming home from a long night of partying. When she and her friends saw me, it was early afternoon. They followed me all the way to my mom's house where I was staying. I had never seen her or her friends around before. We talked for a few minutes and then exchanged phone numbers. I didn't call her after the first time I met her. I had lost her phone number, so she looked for my number in the phone book. My number was unlisted but she found someone in my family who gave her my number. That's when we started talking. She came to my house and for me, it wasn't love at first sight. She was just another girl.

In the beginning, I made her believe I was such a good guy. On our first date, she couldn't find a babysitter, so I suggested she bring her baby. Her baby wasn't feeling good that night and as we ended our date I stopped at a pharmacy and bought the baby some medicine. I bought myself an apple juice. I bet she thought I was so sweet. That was something I did all the time—I played a role until I knew I had the girl on the end of my string, and then I knew I didn't have to play it anymore.

After going out a few times, Blanca told me she had a boyfriend, but I didn't really care at the time. I kind of threw it back at her by asking her, "why are you going out with me if you are seeing someone else?" But not only was she talking to someone else but she was actually engaged to the guy (Oscar.) I didn't really care one way or the other. It wasn't like I thought she was anything special at the time anyway.

I showed my real self after a few months into my relationship with Blanca. I began feeling strongly toward her, and that's when I became very jealous and violent. I had real feelings for her, so that made her mine. I wasn't going to let anyone interfere with that. The times we went out, if anyone tried to speak to her, it was the end of the world. I wanted to fight everyone and anyone that tried to talk to her.

As we continued on with our relationship, I began to show more signs of anger and violence. It first started with a push and shove here and there. There was an awful lot of verbal abuse. I had a really disgusting foul mouth. It didn't come from my parents; my parents never cursed in the home. The foul mouth mostly came from being out on the street. I felt that a tough guy could get the point across with that verbal abuse, and if not, I would get physical. It didn't take much to set me off.

## *THE PROPOSAL*

My father always said, if you ever get a girl pregnant, you will marry her. You will be a man of responsibility. So, when Blanca told me she was pregnant, I knew I had to take care of my responsibility. I made the decision to ask her to marry me. Surprisingly, she said yes even after all the abuse. There came a time where she began to question her decision. My mother and grandmother had been asking her if she was sure she wanted to marry me. Three days before our wedding, Blanca tore up our marriage license. I became very angry as I picked up the pieces, I threw them at her and told her that she was going to marry me whether she wanted to or not.

## *DRUG OVERDOSE*

Shortly after our marriage, I had a drug overdose and went to the hospital. It came after days of bingeing on drugs. I collapsed as I walked into our apartment. Blanca called her brother and he came and rushed me to the hospital. Blanca very disappointed filled out the forms at the emergency room. She did not know I was doing drugs all this time. I convinced her it was my first time using cocaine and that I would never use it again. She believed me, but of course, that was all lies.

## *MY ROCK BOTTOM*

Now my life was drinking, drugs, and trying to take care of one small child and a baby on the way. I couldn't keep a job. Our lights were always cut off. Our car was repossessed. There were many nights when we ate baloney sandwiches by candlelight. I was totally irresponsible. One evening, I got home late, she had enough of this behavior. She was angry and she threw my work boot at me. She missed me and hit our daughter in the face. I felt so bad and I had no words to say. I simply just left when she told me to leave. I went to my mother's house. My mother said I could stay as long as I wanted.

Being at my mother's house I felt I was free to do whatever I wanted. I was going out and drinking and doing drugs. After a few months, I suddenly got really sick. I had no idea what was wrong. I had never felt this pain before. I had excruciating stomach pains and a lot of vomiting. I was taken to the emergency room, and the doctor said he thought it was food poisoning and sent me home. The sickness continued. They tested me for an ulcer, and they checked my liver after I said I drank a lot. Everything was negative. They kept sending me home. Two weeks in, I had lost a lot of weight and the room I was in smelled foul, like I was decaying. I cried at night because I thought I was dying. No one knew what was wrong with me.

One day Blanca came to my mother's house to visit me. She thought I was just trying to get her attention, she thought I was faking it to get her back, but she was surprised to see how bad I looked. She could see I looked terrible.

The doctors never figured out what was wrong, but the pain was intolerable. I couldn't keep anything down, not even liquids. I was told to drink a dyed liquid that would help doctors see the inside of my intestines, but I threw it up. Blanca could see I was truly sick.

## *DIVINE INTERVENTION*

After I left the hospital on that occasion, I went home with Blanca. The only place I felt comfortable was in the shower. There, in the shower, I had a very humbling moment where for the first time, I began to pray. I thought, "what do I have to lose?" Even though I was very against anything that had to do with religion. I didn't believe in God. There were times I would take Blanca to church, but then I would leave her there, go drinking, and pick her up afterwards.

But in the shower that day, I was in terrible pain, and I found myself crying out. I said, "God! You see me. Here I am. If you are there, take this pain away from me!" Before this, I couldn't even walk straight because of the pain. After that, I stood up and the pain was gone! I thought, what is this? I couldn't believe it.

After this experience, I told Blanca that I would love to go to church with her that coming Sunday. There were times before that I didn't like Blanca going to church. I was jealous, I thought she was meeting someone there behind my back. But now, I felt I wanted to be at church. I knew that I had a spiritual encounter in the shower and I had felt something I had never felt before. I went to church for the very first time and just started soaking it all in.

## *RELAPSE AND CHANGE*

All that was short-lived because before long, I was back to my old ways. We had some friends over and they filled the refrigerator with all kinds of beer and alcohol. One of my friends asked for another beer and I volunteered to get him one. As I opened the refrigerator door, I looked at Blanca and said I would just have one. Of course, that led to another and another, and by the time I knew it, I was back in the emergency room again because that terrible pain had come back, only this time it was worse.

I finally understood that the pain and the alcohol were connected somehow. Again, I cried out to God to relieve my pain, and again, it went away. And that's when I knew there was something greater in my life, and that I'd had a spiritual encounter for sure. It was time to turn my life around.

I immediately had a foul taste for alcohol and cigarette smoke. I couldn't stand the sight or smell of it anymore. It was very strange. I stayed away from my family, because they always drank when they had gatherings. I just went to church and stayed home. I felt like I'd made a complete turn, and that I was a different person. One day I was this and the next day I was that. My foul mouth changed. The way I carried myself changed. Family members would see me and ask me if I was ok. They would say I just looked different. They were right, everything was different.

# CHAPTER THREE

## *BLANCA: STARTING OVER ALONE*

After I threw the boot and Miguel left, I was very happy. I felt like I had so much peace. I made a phone call to my sister Lydia. I felt that I had to tell someone in my family because they never knew anything and I never talked about it to them, but I felt like they somehow assumed things weren't right. I said to her, "I just want to tell you that Miguel and I are done." And she said, "OK. If there's anything you need, let me know." That was it. I felt completely at peace with him gone.

I was ready to move on with my life. I told myself I could do this alone. I felt like I didn't need him to make it. It wasn't like he was helping me before, anyway. I was ready to start over again, on my own.
 I started planning. I had a job and I was making pretty good mon-

ey, better than it had been. I put my son in daycare, and Briana was going to school. I was going to work every day. Miguel was contributing nothing at all to the family. All I cared about was that I was in a safe place, feeling peaceful, positive. I felt very much like I was going to come out of this situation and everything was going to be all right.

Divorce was definitely going to happen, but I never filed for divorce while he was out of the house. I really think it's because I just didn't have time. I was so focused on working at my job and caring for the kids--all that was so overwhelming. I didn't have money for a lawyer anyway, and I didn't have time for all that paperwork. I was picking up the pieces of my life.

The want for a divorce was always in the back of my mind for sure. I definitely felt it would happen this time. There were other times I told him to leave and he would leave. We talked about divorce, but he always came back. This time I felt peace about getting a divorce. I believed we would not get back together. I just never got to start the process.

In my mind, I felt this time was going to be different for me. He was not going to come back. I never believed he would really change this time. I no longer cared if he changed or not, I just didn't want him back. I was tired of living like that. I didn't care what happened to him. It wasn't my focus anymore.

The bottom line was, I knew I was better off without him. I was happy with the decision I made to get him out. Before, I thought he would come back and he will want to change for the children and me. This time I didn't even want him, so I had no hopes of that. I was just tired and done. No more fighting or letdowns. No more trying to fix it. Emotionally, I was not in the relationship anymore.

## MIGUEL'S ILLNESS

During this time, Miguel was really sick, but I did not feel sorry for him in the least. I thought he was faking and trying to get attention, to get me back. His mom called me many times and said he was really sick, so I finally went to see him. He had lost a lot of weight and looked sick, but I didn't really care. I went and visited but I left after a few minutes.

There was another time he called and said, something is really wrong with me. I got a little scared and went to see him. He had gotten so sick that I saw him lying in the bathtub in the fetal position. He was skin and bones. His color had changed. He was so pale and just didn't look normal at all. He looked like he was in so much pain and couldn't walk. I remember being mad and telling him, "why are you walking like that?" He said, "I am in a lot of pain." I said, "just straighten up and walk right!" I didn't feel sorry for him.

I was getting so upset to see him walking hunched over or making noises; it irritated me. I felt like I had gone through so much pain. Whatever this is, it's nothing in comparison to what he had put me through.

Then he started to smell. It was something kind of like mothballs—a really nasty smell. He would shower, but he smelled. But I still didn't feel sorry for him at all. His mom was concerned but I just thought, he'll get over it. I never thought this was anything deadly. Maybe just a virus or something.

## *THE FIRST SIGN OF CHANGE*

I remember Miguel asked to see the kids so I let him come over to our house. Pretty soon it was getting late and he fell asleep on the sofa. The next day was Sunday. He asked, "would you like to go to church?" It was very weird; I would never expect that from him. Church was never his thing so I was very surprised.

I didn't care which church it was. I was just glad he wanted to go. I was already going to church every Sunday since he was living with his mother. He had never, ever, wanted me going to church alone, and he would never go with me. So, for him to suggest that we go to church was very hard for me to believe.

I really thought he was just doing it for attention or to try to get me back. I thought, he is trying to ease his way back in and church will be his way to do it. Since I knew that he was an atheist and hated anything that had to do with religion, I kept my guard up.

I didn't question it much and I didn't really have hopes of him changing. I did not believe it was real, I did not get excited. I was frightened of setting myself up for failure again. I didn't think that him being in church one time meant everything had changed.

Well, we did go and we drove to the small non-denominational church I was going to. The whole experience was all right. He actually stayed the entire service. He never said he liked it or anything but I could tell that he was a little different. I began to feel sorry for him. He still felt very weak due to his sickness and that's when I started to take his illness more seriously. Although he didn't have the pain anymore, the smell was getting worse. That's when it became more real to me, because I knew he couldn't fake that smell. It just wasn't normal. I allowed him to stay at our house after that.

## *PERSISTENT DOUBTS*

When he told me the story about God helping him in the shower to take the pain away, I believed him. He was walking normal again. He started eating. He didn't throw up anymore. He started to get better. But I still didn't believe it would make him stop drinking and smoking.

I did believe God took his physical pain, but I had my doubts about the rest. My thoughts were that the only reason why he hadn't been drinking and doing drugs was because he was sick. What happens now that he's not sick anymore? The real test had not come yet. I did not believe he was free from his addictions.

I was right. One evening we had some friends over and they brought beer and alcohol. He volunteered to get some beers from inside and saw the beer in the refrigerator. I thought, here we go again. He took a look at me, I remember him asking me, "should I drink a beer with my friends?" At that point, I didn't care what he did. I didn't want to babysit him. I wasn't going to try anymore.

I had given up on our marriage. I wasn't going to make any decisions for him, because in my mind, I was on my own anyway. Drinking beer was up to him. Before, he never asked me if he could have a beer—why would he even ask me now. Of course, he got sick again after drinking that beer, and I could see I was right to have my doubts.

So I thought, nothing has really changed. I don't remember him promising anything, but my hopes were not high. My guard was up. I felt like I had the upper hand. He was there, but I didn't care. I knew he would fail me again.

## *MORE SIGNS OF CHANGE*

That day we had friends over and he asked me if he could have a beer was the last time Miguel ever drank. But I never put my guard down. He seemed not to be drinking anymore, but I watched his actions. I knew what to watch for. I was ready for him to yell, scream, not show up to work, not show up to the house. I was waiting for shoving or pushing, and I was waiting for his foul mouth to start again.

As I waited for the worse, he made a move I would have never expected. I remember him getting on his knees and saying he was sorry for everything he had ever done to me. It was very sincere. This was something he had never done before—the word "sorry" was not in his vocabulary. I was amazed.

But yet again, I still kept my guard up. I didn't give in to believing it was real. He started looking for a job, going to every temporary agency he could find. He followed through and went to fill out applications. He would stand in line and wait for work. He started showing me by his actions that he was trying. He was doing it all on his own. I didn't ask him to do anything. Then he made the greatest action that made me rethink how I felt. Out of desperation, he grabbed a shovel and walked all the way to a place where lots of day laborers would gather for work. Here was this college educated man with a shovel in his hand ready to provide for his family! All I could think was, WOW!

His language began to slowly change and he stopped disrespecting me. He also began to carry on conversations with me. Conversations about what he felt he needed to do as a husband and a father. He followed up with job offers and he kept going to work without missing a beat! He was even going grocery shopping with me and doing other things he never did.

He was making a lot of small changes. He had stopped hanging around with the people he would normally hang around with. I could tell he was really making an effort. I was done nagging. I was really amazed, and he was doing this all on his own.

## *THE NEXT STEP*

One day, I decided to bring it to a test. I told myself, if he wants to make this work, then he has to take ALL the responsibility. If he wants to be the husband and the father, then he needs to take on everything. I was always in charge of paying bills, daycare, and putting food on the table. I did all that while he was out drinking and doing drugs, but now I was ready to let him take on the responsibility of the man of the house. I wasn't sure if he could handle it. But I knew that I had to give it all to him.

It was a challenge because I had to allow him to be in control of our finances. If something didn't get paid, he had to worry about it, not me. I was not going to nag anymore. The bills were there for him to see and pay, not me. I wasn't going to take that responsibility anymore. He had to just be in charge of it all. The lights did get cut off at some point from time to time, but by that time, I already had seen a huge change in him. He was trying, without me nagging.

I had to allow him to be the head of our household and slowly but surely, he did it when I let him do it. I let him take on the stress that had been mine for so long. I said, "you want to be here? OK, here you go!"

It was so hard. It took so much from me to let it go. I had already decided that I would do it on my own. It was so hard to let him take over. If he didn't come through, it would be even more hurtful. I didn't want to take the risk. I didn't want to go back to my old lifestyle. I had never trusted him with the family load before. I cried and said, I can't believe I am doing this, but this is it! You're responsible now.

## ESTABLISHING TRUST

At first, I was so scared to give him the responsibility. What is he going to do with the money? Will he really use it to pay bills? Before, if he had any money, he always spent it on alcohol and drugs.

We were both working together as a team but he was still the one responsible and took care of the household. It had been about five to six months from the day he sat in the tub and asked God for help with his sickness, to the day where he was taking on responsibilities for the family. We were making small advances but things were looking promising.

There was no more violence, no more cursing. His anger started to go away. He stopped pushing and shoving me. I could tell he was very serious about his change. Something happened in that bathroom when he cried out to God. I just know it. He had started to see how ugly he had been to me. He examined himself very closely during the time he was very ill. I think that's when he realized he'd lost his family. He could see that I didn't care when he was sick. It became so real to him.

I finally reached a point where I felt I could trust him. We would sit down and talk about our finances. We would come up with plans on how to take control of our money. We still had problems. We were very far behind on our bills and our other car was repossessed. We had a lot of financial stress, but he stayed sober. He did not have a relapse.

We were actually beginning to be a normal couple and it was so hard because we had never been "normal" before. Now he had to think like a sober person. Now he was seeing and feeling everything without being under the influence—how could he cope with his feelings without chemicals? We were doing things together, like normal people. It was what I always wanted and to me the biggest thing was that we were doing it together.

## *GOOD INFLUENCES*

It was really important that we got rid of all the things that were negative to us, including a lot of friends who were still drinking and doing drugs.

Miguel's mother stepped up a lot. She told him, "if this is the kind of life you want then you need to change and think about your future". She was important and played a huge role in his change. Our pastor was very important as well. He walked him through his life, and showed him how to change. He needed a positive man's perspective to help him through it. As he met with our pastor more and more, he was able to better himself on a daily basis.

One of Miguel's uncles also encouraged him to make changes. His uncle had made many changes in his own life as well; he was just as bad with alcohol and drugs. He was able to encourage Miguel to make changes—that was a huge influence. Sadly, after many years of sobriety, his uncle relapsed and went back to drinking. Miguel was devastated but he stayed the course and now his uncle looks up to him for staying sober.

I needed a lot of support too. Especially after all that Miguel had put me through. I just wanted to have friends to talk to. I had no friends. I was too focused on trying to make it in life. So I had our pastor's wife and some great church friends who began to encourage me and speak life into my situations. They always told me that I was better than any bad situation.

At one point they asked, "why did you put up with so much?" And even though they didn't really know the extent of what I was truly living, they said I was better than this and that I didn't have to live like that anymore. They encouraged me to put my trust in God. I was truly blessed by all their love and support and it truly made a huge impact in my life.

# CHAPTER FOUR

## MIGUEL: BEGINNING MY RECOVERY

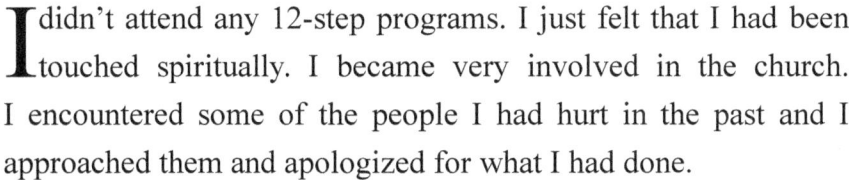

I didn't attend any 12-step programs. I just felt that I had been touched spiritually. I became very involved in the church. I encountered some of the people I had hurt in the past and I approached them and apologized for what I had done.

I cleaned my house. I rid the house of alcohol and I stopped associating with the people we would spend our time with. We took out of our home the things that didn't belong there—all the things that were reminders of my past. No more bad choices, no more bad people. No more drugs, no more liquor in the house. It was a complete clearing out.

I realized when we were going to church that there were Connect

Groups where people would meet in homes. There were Bible studies and nights where people would go out and socialize together. We went bowling and did all sorts of things. It was really fun and I wasn't even drinking. It was a whole new way of life. I was amazed. I could have fun without getting into trouble, without blowing all my money, and without going to jail. I could come home and be happy. Wow! I never thought about a life like this.

For years, I thought life was about partying, going from one job to another, and fighting. Now I could see things from a new, sober perspective. I wanted to create a new reputation for myself. As hard as I had worked to intimidate people and outdrink everyone is how hard I wanted to work to have a different kind of reputation.

## *BECOMING A REAL MAN*

When we began to go to church, I met some awesome men that began to speak life into me. My pastor would meet with me and he would speak to me about what a real man is supposed to be like. He said that just because I drank didn't make me a real man. Because I cursed, I wasn't a real man. Going to jail did not make me a man. My father did tell me these things, but he did not hold me accountable. My father did not set boundaries for me.

I bought a lot of books and started reading about how to be a better person, a role model. I learned about how to be a spiritual leader in my home and how to deal with anger and depression. There was so much information out there about life than I could ever imagine. I always knew this was a divine intervention. I felt so much peace within myself. I no longer felt the torment of convincing myself that drugs and jail were a way of life. There was always something better, I just didn't know how to seek it. I just believed the way I was living was just the way it was going to be. Now I know there is so much more to being a man and living a good life.

There was one person who became my mentor. He had tried to speak to me before when I was out being a bad man, but I was not ready to hear him. This person was my Uncle Ozzy. He is one of my dad's younger brothers. My dad has a lot of siblings and Ozzy is second to youngest, so we were raised like brothers.

We did a lot of partying together. There was a lot of drinking, drugs, and women. The one thing that drew me to Ozzy was that he had gone through his own trials and his own spiritual encounter. He found himself in a bad situation where he had to get it right or he would have nothing.

I remember Ozzy started to go to church. He had shared with me how one day he was watching a preacher on television and it was as though that preacher was talking directly to him. He said he got down on his knees and asked God to help him. That was the beginning of his transformation away from living that kind of lifestyle.

After awhile, when he felt strong enough, he came and spoke to me. He shared with me; life doesn't have to be this way. You can be happy; you can be sober and have fun. I was like, "whatever!" I don't need any help! But when I had my encounter, I began to seek him and ask questions. Now I was asking, "what are you doing that's helping you?". He told me that he went to church. It happened to be the same church Blanca would attend.

I started going to this church, getting plugged in and connected with activities that he was doing—men's groups, dinner with him and his wife, go out do things like bowling. I started to see, it is true! I can have a good time and not drink! I grew stronger. He played a huge role in my recovery in the first stages of my change. He would encourage me to read certain books, and to stay in church. He said I needed to stay around a positive environment. So I did!

### *CHANGING MY PERSPECTIVE*

My perception of manhood from my upbringing was, I saw men gathered together drinking. They were loud, they went to work and they came home. Their meals were prepared, their clothes were washed, and home was cleaned.

I grew up to believe men did what they wanted. No ifs, ands, or buts. I grew up seeing that, so my perception of being a man was just that. I thought, I am the man of the house. I get to do what I want and that's just all there is to it. When I got married that's what I expected. When I came home from work, my meal is served, my house is clean, and my lunch for tomorrow is prepared. I come home when I want and then I leave when I want. I am the man of the house. You don't question where I am going.

Now, I discovered that this doesn't make me a man. What makes me a man is I take care of my home. I thought that's what I was doing. I thought that just because I went to work, and acted like this macho guy who brings home the bacon was all I needed to do to be a man. I learned from a bible study that if my wife's 'to do' list was longer than mine, then I wasn't much of a man. My list had to be longer than my wife's because her responsibility was only to be my helper.

I also discovered that there was a big difference between a house and a home. A house is just the physical. Home is what's inside. The reality was this, that I had to be the man of both the house and the home. Up to now, I just had something physical. Where all I was doing was coming to the house. But now from a different perspective, I knew that I was coming 'home', to a family living inside the house. I realized I was not taking responsibility for my family—they are what make my house a home.

When I began to read different books about being a man, and what it is to be a man, I realized I needed to give back 100 percent. I didn't expect to do anything in my home before, but now I was helping with cooking and cleaning. I took a bigger role in my children's lives. Before, I expected my wife to do that. I helped with homework. I didn't realize just how much there was to do, and I wasn't doing any of it before, but now I was trying to participate a lot more.

I had to understand that being a man of the home means I am caretaker of everything. I am now contributing to the home, not just consuming everything that is there. I have to give of myself to my family. It's a completely different perspective.

That is the problem with a lot of the older members of my family. They still believe in the concept of being the man of the house where the women do it all. That is not the way it should be. This is what being a man is—it's about being a contributor, not a consumer. When you contribute, you gain respect from the family and from others. That respect is much better than what I was trying to gain by being that mean, angry person.

Now I don't even have to work as hard. I just play my part of being the man of the house and I don't have to kill myself for it! I learned I couldn't demand respect; I have to inspire people to want to respect me. I do that through my actions, by being a good father and husband and understanding I am the caretaker of my home and family.

## *INTROSPECTION AND MORE CHANGE*

I lost a lot of my friends during my partying times because I was so violent. They just didn't want to deal with me. If we went out, there was always trouble. A lot of them just wanted to go out and have a good time. I on the other hand, wanted to get violent and hurt someone. But there were some times when they did come around, they would offer me beer and drugs but they knew me well enough to know when to leave because I would always end up getting violent and the fun would be over.

Then, later, they started to sense something was different. Everything, including the way I spoke, was different. They were not aware that I didn't drink anymore. I would just tell them that I had decided to do things differently. They would come around or call because they wanted to keep partying, but I didn't want to do that anymore. It wasn't that hard to get them not to come around anymore; I simply just did not want to party anymore and they did. So, a lot of them wouldn't come around anymore. Sometimes I would come across them at the store or somewhere, but I never went looking for them. It was not that hard of a transition.

But now I have had friends from my past who have reached out to me seeking help. That makes me feel really good, that they will call me and say I need help. That means the world to me. "My old friends would call me for help"- who would have ever thought. It shows that they do respect me, but in a good way.

## *THE NEW MIGUEL*

Like everyone else, my father found the new me hard to believe. It was hard to believe I wasn't drinking anymore. I had gone to college when I was still addicted, and got a degree, but I still saw myself as a failure. I didn't think I could go into the field I had studied—electronics engineering. I didn't think I was smart enough. I verbally abused myself. I told myself, "you're just an alcoholic, just a drug addict". I thought, "well, I guess I will just go into construction and not go into the field of electronic engineering". I didn't think I was capable enough.

My dad worked hard to provide us the means to go to college. He wanted me to have an office job indoors, which is an easier life than what he had. But with all the negativity, I felt I was not worthy of it. I just thought I would work construction and that's just going to be my life.

So, my dad started to show me a lot of what he knew in construction, and began mentoring me as a machine operator. I started off as a laborer but he really wanted me to be a machine operator because they brought home more money. I picked up fast, moved up fast, and began to be a machine operator. I began to make decent money. I thought $500 was great, but then I brought home more and more. I thought, wow, I can really do this!

Then came the budgeting and the finance part of my recovery. I didn't know anything about it, because no one ever taught me anything about that. Where do I begin? My dad didn't budget, or maybe he did, but he never taught me. My mom, she thought about it occasionally but didn't know where to start either. None of us knew anything about it.

Little by little, I figured things out. I read books about how to finance. I sought out others who were doing well. I would reach out to my Uncle Ozzy or my pastor. I asked, "how do you manage your money?" They showed me some principles and laid the foundation as far as money management goes. I grabbed info from everyone.

At first Blanca was handling the money and paying the bills. She didn't think she could trust me. She had to build that trust in me that I could handle it. I began to look at the bills, add them up, and budget. Whatever we had left, I would treat my family. It was a huge change. It was different. I had money in my pocket. I never had money before. Before, when I had any money, it went to drugs and alcohol.

## *FINANCIAL RESPONSIBILITY*

It was a challenge at first. I stayed in construction for 10 years. I traveled a lot out of state. Through the years I was making more and more money in the construction field and I began to save some money. Something I had never done before. I kept reminding myself, "I want to be the provider."

In the past, I struggled a lot with money. I was always borrowing and my credit was very bad. We had a huge struggle with finances. Finally, after reading a Scripture that said, "You will lend to many nations but will borrow from none." I decided I didn't want to be a borrower anymore. I was so sick and tired of that. I made a savings account and an emergency savings.

Then the day came when someone asked me if I could lend him some money. I was thinking, sure! I felt so good! Of course, I had that money! That was the greatest feeling. Be the lender, not the borrower. That was really a WOW moment! It felt so good to me. I pushed even harder to want to be even more successful. I could see how I'd lived the part about struggling, but I see it now, and I can help someone in the same situation that I was in. Being a lender was the greatest feeling. Better than drugs and alcohol!

Little by little Blanca recognized that I had control over our finances and she started to slowly trust me in this area. She told me that the responsibility was all mine now. For so long she was the one who was taking my role of the man of the house so letting it all go to me was difficult for her. She was finally able to let me be the man of the house. In this role, I respected her, because she did what she could to handle our finances. I was far from it and I was still developing this role. We were still struggling at times. It was all new to me. But it evolved and I got better and better. At one time, my financial goal was just to make rent. Now I was saving and making all my bills on time.

Things remained a little challenging with our finances but eventually we were able to move away from that apartment where Blanca threw the boot at me into another apartment—it was a brand-new complex. We lived there for about six months. From there, we moved into a three-bedroom rental home and that's where everything changed as far as my transition in life. It seemed like it took a long time to get our finances straight.

## *CHANGES IN THE MARRIAGE*

As far as my relationship with Blanca, things started to change. I started walking away when I was angry. I didn't give Blanca any reason to confront me anymore. Before, just the simple question of asking me where I'd been would set me off. Or the question as to why was I drinking. All of this would always bother me; I was the man of the house. You don't question me. This was my way of thinking.

But now all I ever did was go to work or if I was off from work I would just stay home. Maybe I was at a church men's group, or simply just helping out at church. I never gave her reasons to question me anymore, or assume things about me that were negative.

Even when times got rough with our finances and I would feel frustrated, instead of blowing up I would go outside and go for a walk. I didn't want to repeat my old first reaction which was to curse at the whole world. I was always using foul language. But now things were different. I didn't use any foul language anymore. It was the strangest thing. I don't know how that all happened. I just felt like it was bad for me to talk that way. I wouldn't want my kids to speak this way so I stopped before they picked up on it.

Now I spend most of my time around positive people who don't speak with foul language. I set myself up to have an accountability with those around me to keep me in check. I knew that I had to retrain my mouth but didn't know how. If you were to ask me what helped. I would have to say that the change of my environment had a lot to do with it. Before, the more I cursed, the more respect I had. Now, the more I don't curse and the more I contribute, the better everything got.

## *GETTING ON TRACK AND STAYING ON TRACK*

When our lease was up from the rental home, we decided to try to get a home of our own. Our debt and credit history was very bad. Nobody would give us a chance to buy a home. But in the end, we found a home, and we were able to purchase the home with assistance from my wife's little sister.

It was good that we got the help we did from my wife's sister but I still felt like such a failure. I was not able to provide a house for my family under my own name. The negative thoughts of my past came back to haunt me. "It's because of my past, that's why I'm struggling; I have to suffer the consequences", I would say to myself. I couldn't see the positive from this. I was blinded by all the negativity in my past.

We were out of the rental home and moved in with my father-in-law for a short time in waiting for the closing process of our home. During this process was when I believe Blanca's family really took notice of the change in us. Her family didn't really know the details of what we'd been through, but they knew we were struggling. They didn't know the extent of our problems. I think they just saw a change, like, they're doing OK!

When we finally moved in to our home, more change followed, and it came at a rapid pace. We lived in that home for 10 years. There was a sequence of events that happened in those 10 years that led to where we are today.

Ones of those events, I know had to be planned for me by God. I was working construction and traveled a lot. I was away from my family most of the time. I didn't have family, friends or anything with me, and I didn't like it. There was a moment close to the holidays where I just wanted to be home. It was enough traveling!

I just wanted to be with my family! I began to pray and say how much I wanted to be home. I knew that the only way I was ever going to come home was if somehow God were to intervene. I was right. I was working in New York constructing a golf course. We were knocking down the whole side of a hill using dynamite, and pushing it out of the way with bulldozers. One day I was on the bulldozer, and it was very rough terrain. Suddenly, my back just snapped. I was rushed to the hospital. I had a very badly ruptured disk so they had to send me home. Not the way I wanted to come home but I got to be home for the holidays with my family.

I could not grasp why God would send me home this way but I knew that my prayer was answered and that maybe, just maybe, God was doing something much greater in me than I thought. I was right! God was teaching me how to be humble and very patient. Because I got placed under workman's compensation, I underwent through an ordeal that required lots of patience and humbleness. And on top of that, I was in a lot of pain. In fact, the entire next season in my life after my back injury was very humbling.

When it's workman's comp, just know that you will be going through a long process. I was given a number of steroid shots and underwent lots of physical therapy. My doctor said surgery was needed, but workman's comp did not want to approve the surgery. This went on for about a year or so. The good thing was that even though I was not working, I was receiving a check every week. Not a very big check but at least it was something.

After a year of this I began to feel miserable and I started to feel like

I was falling into a depression. Things felt like they were falling apart all over again in my finances. The check I was receiving was not enough and we were dipping into our savings. I was so angry within myself because things were finally getting better and I just had a major setback. This time it wasn't my doing. It wasn't because of my drinking or drugs. It was a job-related injury. Be careful what you pray for! I wasn't specific enough! I asked for a homecoming but didn't count on getting hurt. It was all very humbling.

I was never put in a position like that before. Then finally, I got the surgery that was needed to fix my ruptured disk. And after another six months for therapy, I was ready to get back to work. The only problem was, I couldn't go back to construction because of all the restrictions. I really struggled with that, because construction was all I knew how to do! So, I thought.

I had a cousin working for an engineering firm at that time and she said I should come see her. She was recruiting for this firm. She set me up an interview and I got hired immediately. I'll never forget that moment. This employer changed my finances drastically and our way of living followed.

# CHAPTER FIVE

## BLANCA: CARRYING THE FAMILY AGAIN

While Miguel was hurt and on disability, all I could do is just continue to encourage him. It eventually began to get very difficult for us financially because our income was cut in half. We were back to the same place where we started financially and it was a challenge. When he came home from out of town to be with us for the holidays, it was a blessing but it was not good financially. Emotionally, he was feeling very depressed, hurt, and unhappy. His self-worth was very low. I just encouraged him daily and told him everything was going to be OK. We didn't know to what extent his back surgery was going to be. I thought it was going to be minor and it wouldn't take long to get back to work. I was a little hard on him, because I thought it couldn't be that bad, just like when he had the stomach illness. I would tell him things like, "just go get the meds or the shots, but don't get surgery." I thought surgery was too much, and I knew that financially he had to get back to work. I had a fear of falling back and going back to where we were, no money to pay for our home and bills. I didn't fear him going back to drinking or drugs, so that really wasn't the issue anymore. It was more the thought of the poverty mentality, losing our home, not paying our bills. All the fears from the past.

## *DEALING WITH SETBACKS...AND ANGER*

We had already set our foundation with ourselves and our family and children. We showed them where we were, we proved that were doing better, we were both working, and trying to do better in life. To have that setback with Miguel's injury was really hard. Setbacks were not an option for me. I found myself forcefully telling Miguel to just get the shot and get the meds and go back to work. So, he would go and get the shot, and it would work, but not for long. Every time we'd go to the doctor, they'd confirm that he needed the surgery. But workman's compensation would not grant him the surgery. He couldn't walk, and he was miserable emotionally. I was a little bit angry. I was getting really tired of dealing with his traumas. Again, as always before, I felt like I had to pick him up. Here we go again.

I didn't want to be in that place any more, being the "man of the house." I had to go back to that again—be the one to provide, pay the bills, and make sure the kids were set. It was like starting all over again, in a different sense. I really didn't want all that responsibility again. I felt like I paid my dues already with this. I was working, and he was getting a disability check, for two years he received his disability check, and I don't know how we did it but we did. We pushed through.

## *SUCK IT UP AGAIN*

We kept our home, and our bills were paid, but it took a lot from us. I learned not to be so prideful and to just suck it up again. I did resent it a little, that I had to take this role again. Physically, he couldn't do anything. Emotionally he was depressed and down on himself so I had to help him through that also. I couldn't be angry for too long because he was already feeling so bad.

Now I had to get him out of that depression. To make him feel better, I would tell him he was smart, and that he could always get an office job. I always told him how smart he was, but in the past, he just didn't always use his intelligence in the best way. After his surgery, and after all the physical therapy, he began to send out his resume to try to get an office job. It was a challenge for him. His experience was construction. That's all he had on his resume. He began to doubt himself. He didn't even feel like he could do an office job anyways, sitting inside all day would be new to him. He was applying and submitting his resume at different places. He would get so excited about it. But then he'd never hear back. He would call me at work just to tell me that he applied for this job and that job! Then he'd call me back again and say, "I never got a call back." I'd continue to encourage him, and tell him that something will come. I had to be so strong for him. And even though I was happy to see him trying, I would hang up and cry. I couldn't be weak around him, because he was already depressed. But I always cried when we hung up that phone.

He was really trying, even when everything was against him, I could see how hard he was working to get an office job. It felt like this was happening to both of us. It was so hard for me as well, just to be strong for him. There were times when I didn't even know what to say anymore. But despite his disability and his mindset, we pushed daily and we did alright.

Then one day, he received a phone call from an agency where one of his cousins worked. They hired him and he took the job at an engineering firm. He was so happy and excited. Finally, an office job! But then, after his first day of work, every single day he would call me and tell me that the job was not for him. He would say, "I am going to quit. I can't do this, I don't even know what they're talking about at times". I would again encourage him and tell him, "yes you can, you can do it. You won't quit." He would then say, "I will go in one more day and then I will quit." We did this for a whole month because he didn't think he could do it. Him sitting all day in an office on a computer was very hard for him. I would repeatedly say to him, "you will not quit." And eventually, he learned to love it and today, he loves his job a lot. He's been promoted several times. To see him where he is now, it's been a success story. Never underestimate your potential.

## *FINDING MY WAY*

For my own support, my family, Miguel's family, my church family and close friends were there for me. One day a friend of mine offered me a position where she was working but I didn't want to take it because I didn't know the field—document control in engineering. This happened while Miguel was still at home. This friend knew my situation at home and she would tell me to come interview because she believed I could do the work. I would tell her no, that I was OK where I was. But she insisted and continued to bug me about it, nonstop. Finally, I told her that I would go for the interview. It was all the way in Houston and I never drive to Houston. Miguel had to drive me. We arrive according to the directions and this was a huge building. I was totally intimidated. I thought, "there is no way I could ever work here!" I went to the interview with such a negative attitude, feeling absolutely sure I wouldn't get hired. I told them I had no experience in this field and basically, no clue about this job.

They took the time to explain to me what all they did in the document control department, and yet, I still had no clue what they were talking about. I was a receptionist at a small clinic. This was way over my head. So, I thought! But I said I was willing to learn. On our way home, Miguel and I talked about the interview the entire trip. He was very supportive and he was telling me that I was very smart and intelligent and that I could do anything I put my mind to do. Sounded very familiar. They called me the same day and offered me the job. They asked me what salary I wanted. I was so nervous; I didn't know what to ask for.

### *A NEW PROFESSION AND A NEW OUTLOOK*
I remember nearly flipping out when they asked me if I'd like $20

an hour. This was around the year 2004, so that was a lot of money for me at that time. I thought wow, this is pretty good! I told Miguel they had just offered me the job and how much they were going to pay me. His reaction was like mine. We were both in disbelief. $20 was something I never thought I could ever make. I called back and told them I would take the job.

The first week I wanted to quit. I was very intimidated. All these people had degrees, they were intimidating; they were engineers. On top of that, my training was very difficult; I was working with two ladies who were training me and then suddenly one of the ladies left, right in the middle of my training. So that left me almost alone and I was overwhelmed. I just wanted to quit! Again, I told myself to suck it up! I had to do this. I said, "OK, I can do it." Then to my surprise, on my first week, I went to a safety meeting and I was asked to speak. I was in this huge conference room with a long table full of engineers and I had to do a safety topic. The evening before, Miguel ended up helping me with the topic and told me what to talk about. I was sweating, I was very nervous! I kept telling myself, "I can do this! I have to do this!"

I did it! Once that safety topic was over, I thought I could conquer the world. It was great after that. I wanted to learn more and I started loving my job. I even started training others that were coming in. I excelled at a rapid pace. Even when I tried to leave the company to interview with another company, my boss counter offered, and said they'd match what the other company was offering me. They were not about to let me go that easy. They loved my work ethic. Slowly but surely, I ended up loving what I did and it felt so good.

I just kept reminding myself and telling myself, "Blanca, you can do it! Stay here, you'll learn it, don't give up." And I didn't give up and everything worked out.

## THERE'S SO MUCH MORE OUT THERE

During this time, I am working and Miguel is home not working due to his back. This work in the engineering field was giving me a lot of self-esteem and I felt very fortunate. I felt like I could do anything, as long as I took the risks and if it hadn't been for me pushing myself, I wouldn't have ever experienced any of this. And even though I was so scared and terrified of saying or doing the wrong thing, I had already overcome so much. It was so good to be working there and to know I could do these things.

I never again had to live the way I had once been living. There is so much opportunity out there. I didn't even know that it was out there; I certainly didn't think I could reach for it. Now I can say, I don't think people realize the opportunities that are out there, or the things they can overcome, if they just take some risks. I honestly don't think people should have to live like I was living, I know I shouldn't have been. No one should be. There is better, I saw that and I knew it. I can't just say it and not know it—I have been there.

I always tell people, you can do better. You don't have to live like this or that. And some people say, no you just don't understand, I can't. But I do understand; people just don't know our story. I get very emotional. If they only knew where we came from. They think oh, you have no worries, you have a nice family, you have a nice house and you have a great job. They don't understand what it took to get here, the sacrifice, the hurt, the pain. If you are living in that pain and mess you don't have to stay there. You can come out and things will always get better, there is no limit. You can go as high as you want to go, it's just up to you, how bad do you want it? How bad do you want to come out of where you are?

That's where I feel people don't realize their own potential, or what they can do in life. So many smart people who don't know they're smart and have so much to offer and so many companies are looking for what they have. So many people looking for hardworking people who are just willing to learn. People don't think they can do it. They think if they don't know the field of work, it's not for them. They say, it's not the job for me, I can't do that. I say yes, you can. I was always taking the minimal because that's what my mentality was telling me, but I didn't know how much more I could do till I did it. There is a lot of fear involved in just stepping out there and I was terribly afraid, but the key is that I was a hard worker and I was willing to learn.

Some people just think they're limited. We are trying to get people just to realize they don't have to limit themselves. After what Miguel and I have gone through, we now see a lot of potential in people, we see them and we think, "you don't have to be where you are. You really can do it." Miguel and I tell people this all the time, "YOU CAN DO IT!"

# CHAPTER SIX

## *MIGUEL: GETTING OFF MY BACK AND ON MY FEET*

I had the back surgery, finally, in 2004. The doctor asked me about my pain level. I told him that I was at about a pain level eight. He told me he could get me at a pain level two, and asked me if I thought I could live with that. He went on to say that I may experience some days where I may not feel any pain at all, but I will never be permanently pain free. "I might live at a pain level two", I thought to myself. I was at an eight, which was terrible. So, I said, absolutely. I'll take the surgery.

The surgery went well and I feel that it helped a lot because before my surgery, I wasn't able to do very many things. Since then I have been able to do a lot more. In the process of recovery, I never gave much thought as to what the painkillers would have on me. I was a recovered alcoholic and drug user, but the painkillers didn't seem to grab a hold of me. When they sent me home, I had a morphine pump connected directly to me and every time I felt pain I would press the button to release the morphine. Then after a few days, they removed it and prescribed me Vicodin. I had never taken Vicodin and didn't know what the side effects were. When I took the Vicodin for the first time, I was hallucinating and it freaked me out. It reminded me of those old days of when I was out there using drugs and doing things I shouldn't have been doing.

I began to tell myself that I can't continue to take painkillers. I wasn't afraid I'd get addicted to the pain pills. I just refused to have to live the rest of my life on pain pills. So, I began to research for other means of coping with pain. It was around that time I came across an article about Lance Armstrong. In that article, he talked about having pain due to cancer and learning to live with it. And so, I thought, I just had to learn to live with this pain. Even in the old bad days, it was a temporary fix to do drugs. I didn't need temporary. If it's just going to be temporary, I might as well learn to live with it.

I embedded that article in my mind and heart. I told myself that I would just have to learn to cope with it. I would have to change the way I did things so I could protect my back and not turn to prescription drugs to relieve the pain and to help me relax.

I tried to do anything to distract myself from the pain. I would do things outside that weren't too physical. I really enjoy working outside in the yard. Meditating and praying a lot would relax me. I would just keep myself occupied and busy before I could even start thinking about my back hurting and needing to pop a pill.

But the times I would feel pain the most was bedtime. I would toss and turn and not be able to sleep due to the pain. I had to place pillows in between my legs just to find that comfortable spot. I really had to educate myself a lot on how to prepare for bed. I tried everything just to cope with my back because I didn't want to turn to pain pills. I had heard a lot of stories about people getting addicted to pain pills and I didn't want to be another statistic. I put it in my mind that I can do all things through Christ who gives me strength. I can do this! Why wouldn't I be able to do this? I had gone through so much more, so why wouldn't I be able to deal with the back pain. I can do it without the prescription drugs. I just had to continue to educate myself and push myself to live a prescription free life.

My back today doesn't hurt excruciatingly, it's more like I will wake up sore. I do my stretches and once my body gets going, I am fine. That's not to say I am not exempt from anything happening. Just the other day, I lifted up a small tank of propane. I lifted it wrong and my back gave out. I should have lifted it differently. There are some things I need to watch out for and be more careful when doing them.

I learned some life lessons from my back ordeal. Just like me having to educate myself on how to do things with a bad back, we must also educate ourselves on how to live a good life when it's bad. We must learn how to do things in a different perspective. The more we train ourselves to do the right thing, we will end up doing the right thing always. I adapted to a life with a bad back. I had to learn to live with it. There are some things in life that will probably never go away but we have to learn to live with it. I have accepted this fact and I have made up my mind to continue even with this thorn in my paw.

## *NEW JOB, OLD MESSAGES IN MY HEAD*

During my recovery from the back surgery, I got hired at an engineering firm. I had a lot of feelings of intimidation at the beginning—I was really on an emotional roller coaster. I could have given up. What was most empowering were just the positive words Blanca spoke into my life. Prior to this, I was spoken of as a failure, an underachiever, alcoholic, druggie. Everyone would say that I was going to end up dead or locked up for a very long time. I always heard I was never going to amount to anything. I carried those words everywhere, causing me to have very low self-esteem.

Some of my family members and friends would say these things about me all my life. I believed them—my family, who knew me, always said I would never amount to anything. Friends would say, "oh, he'll get locked up before anything good happens." I couldn't ignore it-- those words do pierce the heart. You do so much to ignore it, but when I look back, I know it really did hurt.

## *POSITIVE WORDS*

Before, I had things to turn to when I wanted to get those words out of my mind, like violence, drugs, or alcohol. Those things all made me feel great. When I was drunk and violent, I would believe that I was not this lowlife, I would say to myself, "look at me now! I just beat someone up!" I felt that if I did something negative to feed the negativity, I would get a positive feeling out of it.

But I learned very quickly that the opposite of negative words are positive words. Yes, of course I knew they were opposites but I never applied them in the ways that I should have. I learned so much when I began to educate myself on certain principles. There were some positive words that were spoken over me, by my wife, people at church, and even some family members who did say positive things to me. Some of them felt I would overcome all my addictions someday. I also had some friends who saw me as someone who had the potential to be a success.

On the up side, not everyone felt negatively about me. This helped me a lot. It pushed me to learn that I didn't have to let negative feelings get the best of me. Those feelings will not determine and can't determine my future. I began to question, and reflect on certain things I read in the Bible. It all became so real to me. It's so true and real what the bible says, that people will perish because of lack of knowledge. They're just not educated to know otherwise, about the great future they have, and that's how I was too.

For most of my teen and young adult life, I was told I could never do certain things. I didn't know otherwise. But everything changed when I started to ask myself who I was. I started thinking about my capabilities. I kept referring to the Bible; it was the one tool I had that inspired me. So many scriptures that told me otherwise from what I felt about myself and the way God saw me.

## *INSPIRATION FROM THE BIBLE*

Verses in the Bible like, "I am the head and not the tail", "I am a lender, not a borrower", "I am above and not beneath." There were so many scriptures that inspired me. I knew I could be these things because the Bible told me so. So, I placed those scriptures in my heart, deep enough to where the negative things that were in there had no room to be in there anymore.

I sometimes can still hear those ghostly negative words that were spoken over me, but they don't affect me anymore. I use them as fuel to help me help individuals with this same problem. When people come to my home and they tell me, "Miguel you just don't understand what I am going through." I pause for a second and smile. People often think I have everything figured out just because of where I live now and because of all the possessions I have. But they don't see what I see in my home and in my possessions. I see something totally different. A lot of the times they just don't know where we came from or how hard we worked to get where we are today. I am very grateful to be where I am today. Not one day goes by without me spending some time reading scripture from the Bible, it's what gets me going every single day.

## *LIVING MY ACCOMPLISHMENTS*

One day I invited someone to my home who was going through a very bad financial time in his life. He was about to get evicted from his apartment. We started examining the problem together. I had him write down his debt, and write down how much he brings home. We started looking at his money in an honest way and talking about the realities.

In the process, he kept telling me that I didn't understand where he was or how he even got in this situation. I would reply to him, "yes, I do understand." He insisted, "No, you just don't understand." So, I told him, "I want you to look around and tell me what you see." He replied, "You have a beautiful home and one day I will have a house like this."

My point of view, when I look around at my house, is something totally different. I see achievement, I see what I have overcome. I see that I can do all things through Christ who gives me strength. I began to share with him where I came from. He had tears in his eyes and he said, "forgive me Miguel, I never knew this about you." He went on to say, "there's no way you were like that and living that way. You could not have been a person like that and be where you are today."

## *TEACHING OTHERS WHAT I LEARNED*

I told him, "when I say I know where you are, I really, truly do. Now, are you willing to listen?" He said, "yes, I will listen to whatever you have to say." So, I began to teach him. First, I told him that he had to learn to live on the income he was on and not try to live a lifestyle way beyond his means. That was his biggest problem—he was living in a place he couldn't afford. I suggested he go live in some apartments I knew very well. He went to look at the apartments and his response was that he could not live there. I told him, "look man, do you want me to help you get back on your feet or not? There is a season for everything."

"You must adapt to what you have. It's only for a season. Adaptation is the key element for a person. If you can adapt to the income you have now, and educate yourself how to adapt in any situation, you'll learn to survive and you'll be better at it and improve. I have taught you how to budget and now you see that you can really get out of this situation. Desperate times call for desperate measures", I told him. When you're in a humbling state, everything matters. He didn't allow himself to be humbled. He forced himself to want to live at a certain expectation for which he didn't have the means, but all he did was just hurt himself.

I had to tell him that he was doing everything the wrong way. From start to finish. And not just in his finances but everything. He can't fix his finances if he doesn't fix himself first. So, we began to take some personal steps to get him more confident and get his self-esteem at a higher level. If you learn to survive in an environment that you're not familiar with, like where my wife and I were years ago before we changed our lives, you won't be afraid of anything anymore. I know how to survive having nothing, I have been there, and I know how to get out of it.

He went with everything I taught him. He went and lived in those apartments for a season. He got caught up on his debt, when he was so late on his bills before. His credit was hurt but soon after, his credit got better. He got a better job, and saw more finances come in. He moved out of that apartment into something better and progressed. He just needed to make a few adjustments. That's all. And now, this young man is doing great! What a great feeling it is to see someone come out of a situation they never thought they could come out of.

## HELPING OTHERS FIND THEIR WAY

I had another couple that came to us and they were having marital problems. I began by telling the wife, "look at your husband and tell me what you see." She listed all the negative things about him. He drinks, he doesn't spend time with me, he's not a family oriented man. There were so many negative things she had to say about him. So, I went on to ask her, "what do you want to see in him?" And she listed all the good qualities she wished he had.

I went on to tell her, "that first person you described with all the negative things was me at one time. And the good qualities you wished he had, your husband has those qualities. It's in him, he has all those qualities because I was like him once. That's how some people spoke and thought about me. He's more than capable of being the person you want him to be." I asked her another question, "Why are you in this place?" I had her look at her childhood, and think about her upbringing. That probably had a lot to do with it.

Let's fix this. Look at the little you. If you were to speak to that person what would you say? They both shared the things they were sorry about in their lives and they cried. I told them both, "now you know why he/she reacts the way he/she does." They finally told each other things they had never known about each other. It was simply just a lack of communication. It was a lack of looking honestly at the situation and saying, let's fix this, and a lack of conviction to make things right.

It's so inspiring to see someone who was about to separate and be able to help them see beyond the present circumstances and look beyond negative. When they get past it and live a better life, live out their hopes and actually see the positive hopes they had for themselves, it reminds me of where I was in my marriage. I didn't have anyone to speak that into me in the beginning. No one told me I was better than I was. I was just an alcoholic/drug addict. I look back and I wish I had heard someone tell me my worth.

## *ALL THIS WILL BE ADDED UNTO YOU*

Today, people see me as someone who will help guide them through things. I try my best to lead by example. My favorite scripture in the Bible is, "But seek first his kingdom and his righteousness, and all these things will be added unto you as well"- Matthew 6:33. What does that mean? The Kingdom of God is all around us. I want to help those around me, and do what Jesus said to do. It also says in the Bible, "for I was hungry and you gave Me food; I was thirsty and you gave Me drink; I was a stranger and you took Me in; I was naked and you clothed Me, I was sick and you visited Me;

I was in prison and you came to Me." I began to do all these things. The ones closest to me, who knew where I once was, were now seeing someone giving back. Their reaction was, "WOW! I want to do what he does!" Now don't get me wrong, I am not boasting. I was one of those that would say, "I want what that person has", or "I want to be like THAT person". People will always believe what you do versus what you say. If I am doing good things, and not just talking about it, people will believe. They will want to know how they can get to that position and be in a better place. They will see you doing things and they will want to do the same.

I had a friend call me once to ask me where I was attending church. I told him which church I was attending. He said he wanted to go where I was going. He wanted to be involved in all the outreaches that I was involved in, and to me that spoke volumes. People really are watching and listening. It keeps me on my toes. It's almost like I'm truly accountable now. That's the driver for me, it pushes me to be better. I let my actions speak more than any of my words.

## *ACTION AND EXAMPLE*

Through the years I have learned to become more transparent. I'm not trying to be a "holier than thou person." I am not trying to preach and push scripture down anyone's throat. I just let my actions speak louder than my words. I live my life having more of a relationship with Christ rather than in a religious way. How can I expose myself if I'm in a box with a religious mindset? That's not effective to me. We need to reach the lost and have to be amongst those people that are hurting and feel lost.

Some people think I should stay away from celebrations with alcohol present because I am a former addict. But how can you reach people if you can't be around them? I show them that I don't need to drink alcohol in order to have fun. I don't live that way anymore. It doesn't matter if I am with people who are drinking, it doesn't affect me. It's awesome to be on this side and show people how life is without having to drink or do drugs. All I can say is that it's working. I am seeing more and more of my family and friends change their ways of life simply because of my positive actions.

It's so sad that I was misinformed. I was never told not to drink. I was told not to do drugs but the alcohol I was drinking lead to my drug use. I saw drinking and drugs as being fun, violence was about gaining respect, womanizing was about being a player. That was simply because I just didn't know any better. I was being misinformed by the actions and examples of everyone else around me. I took this false approach of life and turned it around for the better. I thought, "maybe if I show these people through my actions that there's a different way in life, then maybe I can gain their respect and maybe they'll change their ways." I did just that!

# CHAPTER SEVEN

## *MIGUEL TODAY: ATTITUDE*

It's been 16 years since I stopped drinking, doing drugs, and being violent. Internally, the biggest change in my life has been my ATTITUDE. In my earlier days, my attitude was, "this is just the way life is." My attitude toward certain things had to do with my surroundings and the environment I was in. I believed that the same people around me believed life was just this way as well. Life for a man was about drinking, fighting, and womanizing. Our attitudes were all the same about life as we knew it.

So, my biggest challenge was changing my attitude. I thought that If I could just change my attitude, then I could achieve so much more. I was progressing and becoming a better person, but a lot of times, the old mentality crept in, telling me, NO, you can't do this.

But I would work to overcome it. My attitude became, Yes, I can. I learned that my attitude was a decision and my decision was to continue on the path where I was seeing results and seeing that things are possible if I just put this mentality of being a bigger, better person into practice. I always felt like I could fight my way through anything, but in a very negative way. I was always fighting for the wrong reasons in the wrong way. When I stopped doing all that, everything got better.

Now I feel I can conquer and achieve things in a so much more positive way. That word 'conquer' can mean a lot of things, but that word meant something different to me at one time. It meant, fight and use violence to scare people so I can get what I want. Now I view it as a positive thing, as overcoming my challenges and being a better person. My attitude is totally different today. That's my greatest change and achievement over these last years.

## *THE FUTURE*

One day a good friend of mine asked me where I see myself in the future. I thought about that for minute because I feel that I can be anything I want to be. We all should feel that we could become anything we want to become. So, because of everything I have accomplished from where I once was, to where I am now, if I could become a public motivational speaker, that would be my dream. Today, I get invited to speak at churches and prisons. What a privilege it would be to do that full time, to help educate individuals on how to come out of a life style of drugs, alcohol, and violence.

To help individuals in those areas would be a huge blessing to me and to the families of those people. I wouldn't just be helping one person when I do this, I would be helping everyone around that person as well. That's something I noticed in my life. When I changed, so did the people around me. My thought is this: The only way we are going to fix the society is if we fix the individual first.

My hope is to take this book and the messages in it and bring it to people who are in the same circumstances I once was in. I want to teach people how to find their way out. I feel there are many places this book could do the most good. I can see myself in juvenile detentions, prisons, and rehabs. Perhaps even among homeless shelters. I might have ended up homeless had I not gotten off this path of destruction. I can see myself in any environment where people need to rebuild themselves—it's open to so many places.

## *BEING HONEST ABOUT THE PAST WITH THE KIDS*

I haven't begun to open up to my kids about my past until just recently. When I began to see they're getting older and beginning to find themselves and discover who they really are, I began to share with them a lot about alcohol, drugs and the party life. A lot of my daughter's friends are drinkers and do drugs. I told her about my experiences and how I would hate for her to fall into that trap. I want it to become something they will look at and see my bad choices and decide not to go that route.

Even about sex—there have been a few scary moments in my life where I was tested for diseases I didn't even know existed. When the health department comes looking for you and wants to test you right away because of an outbreak, that's a scary moment, but I'm the one that placed myself in that situation. I tell them not to do these things, because it could happen to them. I tell them that the sin they commit today can affect the rest of their life.

If you're living a sinful life, partying and drinking, you could get in a car accident and your life could be altered forever. You have to think very deeply about what you're doing. I did certain things that affected my life. If I think back to high school, had I not spent a lot of that time skipping school and drinking and doing drugs, I could have become a doctor, lawyer, rocket scientist, or anything I ever wanted to become. Who knows what I could have become. Things may have been very different. I made all the worst choices for my life from a young age and it took me so long to find my way back.

I made sinful choices that changed my life in that moment. I want them to have that picture in their minds, that what they do can affect their lives. I try to speak life to them as much as I can. Every day I send them a text and a scripture to wish them a good day. I want them to know I am thinking about them and I want what's best for them. I am speaking life into their lives, so they don't fall into the same traps as I did.

### *RAISING A SON*

What kind of man am I raising? First and foremost, I want him to be God-fearing. And what is God-fearing? Here is an example. When you are driving down the freeway and you're driving as usual, maybe a few miles faster than the speed limit. Then on the on ramp you see a police car making his way on. You know what happens? You see the cop and then you change everything about your driving. You slow down, you watch your speedometer, you check to see where the cop is. Now your attention is focused on that police car. Then the police car goes off the next exit ramp, and you go back to normal driving. Right?

Whenever there is a higher authority placed in your path, there's always some kind of fear, but then when that authority is gone, you're back to yourself. When you place God first, knowing God is watching always, you become watchful and you become careful of how you're living all the time, not just some of the time, but all the time. God is all-knowing and he will be there wherever you are. Knowing this brings fear into people. So, I continuously express to my son to be a God-fearing person. That fear will help you walk a straight line and in a manner that is pleasing to God and the people around you. Then people will respect you in a real way, not the way I thought respect was, which was by fighting people and intimidating them.

If my son is a God-fearing person, he will want to live a life of excellence—not perfection. No one is perfect. Only God is perfect. But if he can try to live in excellence, there will be no room for failure. Perfection leads to failure, which is why people stop trying to live right. But if you try to work things in excellence, then you don't set yourself up to fail.

Try to make sure your work is always excellent. If you're planning to do something and you're planning to cut corners, just don't do it at all. My son should be a man of his word, do things he says he is going to do, and have a good plan to do it in excellence.

I am trying to lead him by example. If he can see me work hard and see that I am doing everything in excellence, then, chances are he will want to do the same. If he sees that I'm a God-fearing husband and father, then chances are he will be the same. I believe that if I continue to lead him in that way, chances are he will follow and he will have a pretty good life as a father and a husband someday.

So far he's been very successful, my son. Everyone says he's the total opposite of what I was at this age of 17. I am so grateful to hear that. That means I have done a great job as a father. I always feared of him turning out to be even worse than I was, but he is not any of those things. At 17, I was drunk and passed out somewhere living in a manner that wasn't pleasing to anyone. I thank God every day that my son is nothing like that today. Today I live a life of purpose and reason. I know that teaching people is truly my calling in life and teaching my children to do better than I did is the most important thing to me.

# CHAPTER EIGHT

## *BLANCA TODAY: A DRASTIC CHANGE IN MY HEAD*

There's been a drastic change in my head over the last 16 years. It's been the most drastic change of all that's happened, more so than Miguel's sobriety. FORGIVENESS! I think the most important change for me is forgiveness. Being able to forgive is not about forgetting, but if I can't forgive then I am carrying so much bad stuff.

Letting go is letting God do a new thing. But in order to do that, you have to know your value as a woman. You can't let go unless you take that step. It took for me to educate myself, surround myself with women who will encourage and educate me, speak life into me. I have to know I am not alone in this and know that God created me wonderfully. I am hand-picked. Knowing my value, and setting the bar high is important. I have to live life just like God created me, I am fearfully and wonderfully made. That's how I live life, choosing that and not settling for anything less—like the life I was living before with Miguel. If you know your value, and that you are chosen by God to do wonderful things in life, there is no way you can live a life like that.

I believe God put great effort in making every individual, and that knowledge takes me to a whole other level. I don't have to settle for anything less. I can't allow myself to be abused in any way. It's not acceptable to me or to God. We are not put here in this world to be abused by anyone.

Another huge part is to stop seeking approval from others. I had to learn to stop that because placing so much importance on the approval of others is a very bad thing. It put a dent in my life, seeking approval from friends and everyone. I lost my identity. I'm free of that because I found myself and I know who I am. Now I walk in freedom and confidence. I don't have to seek approval from anyone. I have to live the life God has given me and know I am strong, talented. I am courageous. Every woman has that, it's just about discovering it. When you discover it, you will not allow yourself to be treated in any way but with respect. No man is worth losing your self-respect.

### *FINDING WOMEN TO SPEAK LIFE INTO YOUR LIFE*

It's a must that you have other women speak life into you,

encourage you and support you. Women who have been there and you can see the fruit in them. Let them show you what they're overcoming and the new thing they have in their life. Don't listen to the advice from women who are living with abuse and addiction and not trying to change it. Change your environment to include people who support your new attitude about your life instead of keeping you from doing and thinking of the things that you are trying to get away from.

I know what it's like to be insecure and to feel unworthy. I try so hard not to judge, but also to be wise. It's so important to choose the right circle of friends. I have a lot of friends now who encourage me. You have to have people who encourage you and support you. I'd go so far as to say my friends are better than me. I want them to be better so I can keep striving. That's who I want to be around, people who can lift me up to another level. What is my purpose in life? What am I designed to do in this life? Women don't know what their purpose in life is, and what their plan is. Finding your purpose is the most important thing. I want to be around women who are also looking for their purpose in life and they are trying to improve themselves. You can't do that when you are in an abusive relationship.

I try to live in excellence every day. I try to be better every day, not just when it's convenient for me, but to live in that way every day. Simple choices, like just a choice to be happy. It's a choice you make daily, not just when things are good. You have to strive to be happy daily, even if things are going wrong. Are you going to ruin your day because things are going wrong? It's so hard but so easy.

I choose to be happy and wake up and say, what will I choose to be today? Happy, sad? Angry, disappointed? I put in the effort to make the right choice every day. I stayed with Miguel because of his choices to make his life better. If he had gone back to his old ways, we would not be together. I will never go back to that life.

Definitely, I would not stay with an abuser. The red flags were everywhere—I wish I would have moved away from the beginning when I saw them, but I stayed because it was the way I felt about myself back then. I was naïve and scared. As soon as you see red flags, address them. I definitely would not have stayed—don't stay.

You get to the point where either he's going to kill you or you're going to kill him. Any kind of abuse is not acceptable. It was my own low self-esteem at the time and the lack of people to direct me to do better that kept me there at the time.

No one took the time to talk to me. Nobody asked, are you OK? And if you ask and a woman says yes, she's OK, check deeper! Take the time to notice the signs. No one did that for me. I felt like nobody cared. I was trying to figure things out all alone in life. I tried to fix it myself, but his problem was not for me to fix. He was the only one who could fix it, as much as I wanted to, he had to be the one to fix it. Had Miguel not stopped using alcohol and drugs, I would have left. No one should stay in a relationship like that.

### *RAISING MY DAUGHTER*

I spent a lot of time with my daughter and I gave her my full attention. I definitely sheltered her--maybe too much. I am afraid that because I sheltered her so much, now she wants to do things that make me worry. I'm grateful I could hold her close. I always tell her that she can do anything she puts her mind to. She says, "Mom, you think I can do this?" I say, of course! And she says, "you just say that because you're my mom." And I say, "I say it because I believe you can do anything." She says, "Mom, for real, what do you think?" And I say, "for real! You can! Anything you set your mind to do."

Self-respect—how do you teach that? It's all about how you carry yourself. If you have self-respect, everything will fall into place. Respect your mother and father, especially when it comes to your friends. If you don't show respect for your parents your friends will not respect you. I teach her to value herself as a woman, and to look for the right friends. I want her to hang around with friends who will encourage her, speak life into her, want the best for her.

The right friends are not just people who will tell you what you want to hear. So sometimes we get heated. I tell my daughter, "I can say these things because I am your mom, and if I can't teach you and correct you then you won't survive in this world." She's easily offended by the way I talk to her but as a mother, I have to lead her and teach her these things, because if I don't the world will, and they won't be nice about it. I want things to be done right and in order, and I am teaching her that.

Now she's 21, I see more maturity in her. Our talks are now more from woman to woman. We talk a lot about her dating. I tell her to make sure the guy she picks is living right and treats her as a lady.

The girl I am raising is different from me because she's happy, she's confident, and she's very vocal. She doesn't keep things inside like I did. She expresses herself. She's a fighter. She's very protective over her family. She asks a lot of questions and she's very open, which I was not. She chooses things I never did---she knows what she wants. I didn't know anything about life. She has dreams, which I did not. I see a lot of me in her now, she's caring and loving and reaches out to her friends who are in trouble and brings them to our house so that we can mentor them. She says, "Mom, can you talk to so and so? They're going through something." She has a big heart for people. She's been empowered in ways I never was. She will have the tools to handle her life very differently than I did. She values herself and she knows how to expect others to value and respect her as well.

# A LETTER TO MY FORMER SELF

My childhood and young adult life was about living with no boundaries, living only for myself and for the "high" I got from drugs, alcohol and controlling others through verbal intimidation and physical abuse. No one stopped me, no one believed in me, and no one taught me that manhood was about protecting and providing for my family and about finding my true purpose and living it out. I nearly destroyed my mind, my body and my family before I began to learn there was a way out of the degrading, purposeless life I was leading. I didn't realize that all along, I had the strength and the ability to do better for my family and myself. If I had realized it sooner, I would have spared myself years of pain and despair.

I wrote this letter to my former self because there are many others who don't know they can find their way out no matter how low they've gotten. I found my way by opening myself to a new, positive way of thinking, and my former self would never believe how happy, healthy and fulfilled I am today, living out my true purpose with my family next to me and my future before me. It's my hope that sharing this letter will give you the faith to keep trying, because if you have faith in yourself, you'll find your way out of anything.

Dear Miguel,

Looking back over the years, I have realized how much you have grown. You have been through some really rocky times in your life, yet somehow you managed to keep the faith. There were days when you hit rock bottom and didn't think that you could face the day, but you kept on no matter how hard things were or how bad things were going.

You were not always good at being a positive person even when things were falling apart. I think you hid far too much and kept your problems to yourself. You guarded yourself from others and pretended that everything was all right when it wasn't. You were afraid of opening up and being vulnerable to others. You were scared of what they might think. Because of your reputation, you didn't want people to think you were soft.

But now, I see a man who has prospered in every area of his life into what he was meant to be. You finally decided to open up and show your true self to the world. For so long, you kept your true self hidden because you didn't like what you saw or you thought that who you were was not valuable or unique.

Why did you think this?

Was it because you could never let go of the negativity that was spoken over you?

Why did you ever let someone take away your self-love?

I guess you didn't know any better.

Over the years, you struggled so much and all you did was blame yourself, which made things worse.

I wish that you could have seen that your internal struggle was a sign that your true self was being suffocated because you wouldn't let who you were really shine to the world.

You tried to be everything you thought you were supposed to be and you didn't give much thought as to what you were meant to be. All you cared about was how an act of evil might make others proud of you, but you didn't truly think long and hard about what you wanted out of life for yourself. You always thought about others before yourself.

Today, I am so very proud of you.

In the past year, you have grown more than you ever have and you have never been happier. You no longer wonder why you are the one who never seems to get a chance to move forward. Now you understand, you're the one who moves yourself forward. It's not about the others, it's about you.

Why?

Because you listened to your heart! Finally, after all these years!

Turning to the church and becoming a leader in the church is the best thing you've ever done, and you know it. What started as just an idea turned into the great fulfillment of your life's purpose. You feel more alive again and turning to the church gave you a glimmer of hope that you could do something you really have a talent for. You're being true to yourself—this is the way to a fulfilling life. Not drugs or alcohol. Finding yoru true purpose in life is better than any "high" in the world.

Now life is about making people feel that they are victorious and not victims. The hardest decision you have ever made was walking away from your past. I remember all those nights that you cried with your head buried in God's presence asking him for answers.

You finally realized that this is your life and the only one who is going to be able to make you happy is YOU.

Not Blanca, not your kids, not your friends, or your family.

YOU.

Now you know what you're capable of and you're stronger than any chemical you have ever put in your body. You let go of your past and created a new present and a new future. Your future is bright because you're not struggling inside anymore—You know your purpose and nothing will stop you from fulfilling it.

Miguel

# A Letter to my Former Self

# A LETTER TO MY FORMER SELF

The entire journey of my life has taught me that no matter how hopeless and desperate I am or will ever be, there is a way out. When I was younger, I didn't have any sense of my own self worth. No one showed me how to create a good future for myself, and I made a lot of painful mistakes. I wish that I could have known back then how much better my life could be. I look back at the days when I was living with a violent man with two children in an apartment with no lights, and I see a woman who didn't know what she was capable of accomplishing.

I know there are many who are living in my old shoes right now, feeling the pain I once felt. I wish I could have known how wonderful my life would become. I had to make some big changes in my thinking, but I did it. I'm writing this letter to my former self, and I'm saying the things I wish someone had told me to fill me with the hope and strength to never give up on my family, my future, and myself. If you think there's no way out of your current situation, no matter how terrible it may be, let this letter give you the faith you need to move forward.

Dear Blanca

I am writing to you because I love you so much. You are now 41 years old. There are so many things I would like to say to you. First, I want to start by saying that I am very proud of you. You have overcome fear, anger, betrayal, sadness, overwhelming heartbreak, loneliness, bitterness, confusion, rejection, abandonment, hopelessness, physical pain and darkness.

Losing your mother at a very young age was always unfair to you and you longed every day to get a glimpse of her. Your heart had been broken and it was something that you thought would never heal. Through the highs and lows you needed her. You have learned to be a great mother even when you didn't know the love of a mother. I want you to know that your mom would be very proud of you. I know she loved you with all her heart and one day you will be with her in Heaven.

The person who you have become is strong enough and wise enough to make it through anything and everything. I want to tell you to try harder and stay focused and never give up when the unthinkable comes your way. You will have many more experiences you never imagined. You will have heartaches and pain but always remember where your strength comes from. Trust in God and give it all to Him.

I want you to know that you are never alone. I know you have struggled with many things in your life and sometimes you have felt that you are not enough but the truth is you are more than enough. You have so much to share and you are surrounded with so much love. Love has gotten you to where you are today.

I want you to know that your life is important. Always remember to take the time to learn as much as you can from those who know more. It's okay if people do not understand the choices that you have made and will make, because it's not about them. You make the decisions that are right for you now, and you trust yourself to know what you're doing. Always remember that some people do not know what it's like to be in your shoes. You don't always have to be strong. You have been broken time and time again and you have survived. You have discovered that trusting God is worthwhile and that He is who He says He is. He has carried you through it all. Don't ever forget who you are and where you came from.

You have been made whole. You are a jewel. God does not make mistakes. Today marks a very special day in your life and that is because you have chosen to live life in freedom. I want to tell you how courageous you are by writing this book.

I love you very much, I am who I am today because of you, and I love who I am today.

Blanca

# ABOUT US

Miguel and Blanca Quinones together along with their two beautiful children Briana and Isaiha have discovered their calling into ministry and founded Kingdom Church. With more than 15 years of ministry experience, their life became a walking demonstration of Mathew 6:33 where seeking first the Kingdom of God became a life style.

Miguel serves as the Senior pastor of Kingdom Church. Pastor Miguel loves people and he strives to become a better person every day so that he can better others. God has given him a mission to disciple the church to empower the world by reaching the lost, disciple the hungry, inform to transform and Empower ALL. His greatest joy is to see people who are facing great challenges end up as victors and not victims.

Blanca strives to be an example of a virtuous woman—a woman who is yielded to God in every area of her life. Blanca humbly serves as her husband's helpmate. Blanca continues to aim toward and produce excellence in all of her ministry opportunities. She has a heart for people and is a committed prayer warrior. Her life is dedicated to living by example and encouraging woman how to live up to their full potential in Christ.